100 MORE THINGS

EVERY DESIGNER NEEDS TO KNOW ABOUT PEOPLE

SUSAN WEINSCHENK, PH.D.

New Riders

VOICES THAT MATTER™

100 MORE **Things Every Designer Needs to Know About People**
Susan M. Weinschenk, Ph.D.

New Riders

Find us on the Web at www.newriders.com
New Riders is an imprint of Peachpit, a division of Pearson Education.
To report errors, please send a note to errata@peachpit.com

Acquisitions Editor: Nikki Echler McDonald
Production Editors: Tracey Croom and Maureen Forys
Development Editor: Jeff Riley
Copy Editor: Gretchen Dykstra
Technical Editor: Tara Long
Proofreader: Patricia Pane
Compositor: Maureen Forys, Happenstance Type-O-Rama
Indexer: Jack Lewis
Cover Design: Mimi Heft
Interior Design: Maureen Forys, Happenstance Type-O-Rama

ISBN 13: 978-0134-19603-9
ISBN 10: 0-134-19603-1

9 8 7 6 5 4 3 2 1

Printed and bound in the United States of America

ACKNOWLEDGEMENTS

Many thanks to all the readers of the original *100 Things Every Designer Needs to Know About People*. Your enthusiasm, comments, and ideas gave me the inspiration to come up with *100 More*!

DEDICATION

This book is dedicated to my friends and family, who were patient with me and helped me with lots of other tasks so I could concentrate on the writing of this book.

ABOUT THE AUTHOR

Susan Weinschenk has a Ph.D. in psychology and more than thirty years of experience as a behavioral scientist. She is a consultant to Fortune 1000 companies, start-ups, government agencies, and nonprofits. Her clients call her "The Brain Lady," because she applies research on brain science to predict, understand, and explain what motivates people and how they behave.

CONTENTS

HOW PEOPLE READ AND INTERPRET INFORMATION

HOW PEOPLE ARE INFLUENCED BY STORIES

HOW PEOPLE RELATE TO OTHER PEOPLE AND TO TECHNOLOGY

HOW CREATIVITY INFLUENCES DESIGN

HOW PEOPLE INTERACT WITH INTERFACES AND DEVICES

THE DESIGNER AS BEHAVIORAL SCIENTIST

You wake up in the morning and while you sip your coffee, you slip on your headset. A few gestures with your hand and fingers and you are skimming the news and your calendar on the screen that has appeared in front of you. As you walk to the train to go to work, you run your hand down your arm to call someone at your office.

When you get to work you might spend some time in the immersive room. Data appears on a screen, you hear sounds, and feel pulses through the vibrating floor, or a vest you have put on over your clothes. Your unconscious processes these sensory data so that you can make decisions. That's not so far in the future. That's what is about to become mainstream in the next 1–2 years.

This is a great time for designers—there are so many things that can, and need, to be designed! We still need software and websites and mobile apps, and now we also need to design how people will use technology that lives in clothing, headsets, and robots.

Technology is growing and changing, and what we know about people has also exploded. When I wrote the first *100 Things Every Designer Needs To Know About People,* it was 2011. I had summed up the essential information on what designers need to know about people in those 100 things. If you had asked me then if I thought there were another 100 things people need to know, I would have probably laughed and said, of course not!

But a lot has happened in the last four years. Our understanding of the brain and the body has exploded almost as fast as the technology has exploded. Now we know that:

- How we read online is different than how we read text on a page.

- We are not born with brains that know how to read—our brains repurpose other areas of the brain to learn how to read.

- Our unconscious processes big data better than our conscious mind does, and we can actually use something called sensory addition to feed data to the unconscious.

- Our peripheral vision decides where our central vision should look.

- Older people aren't slow to learn and use technology because they can't remember, but more because they aren't confident about their memories.

- People who are blind can see by hooking up a camera to their tongues.

And, well, 94 other amazing things.

I hope you enjoy this book as much as I've enjoyed researching and writing it. I can't wait to see what we all design in the next few years. And I hope that this book will help you design so that your creations fit the way people learn, work, think, and play.

Susan Weinschenk, Ph.D.
Edgar, Wisconsin, USA
July 16, 2015

HOW
PEOPLE
SEE

Recent research offers exciting insights into how people see and how the brain interprets visual data. Now, instead of arguing about opinions, you can present the latest industry findings on everything from shapes to color to visual appeal when you present your designs.

PEOPLE PREFER CURVED SHAPES

Have you ever wondered why clients always prefer logos with curves rather than more daring and modern logos with interesting angles? Have you noticed that your favorite smartphones, tablets, and laptops tend to have rounded corners? What's the big deal with those curves and rounded corners?

People prefer objects with curves—a preference that's evident even in brain scans. This field of study is called neuroaesthetics.

DOES THE COUCH HAVE CURVES?

Moshe Bar is the director of the Cognitive Neuroscience Laboratory at Massachusetts General Hospital. He and his team used images of everyday and abstract objects to see if people had a preference for objects with curves. In one of their early studies, Bar and Maital Neta (2006) showed people 140 pairs of objects. Some objects were concrete, such as watches or couches (the A objects in Figure 1.1), some were abstract (the B objects), and some had both curves and edges (the C objects). The C objects acted as baseline controls.

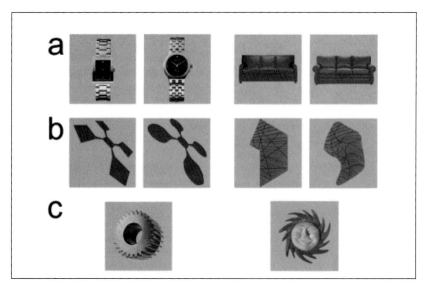

FIGURE 1.1 Original images used by Moshe Bar (http://barlab.mgh.harvard.edu/publications.htm).

People gave higher "liking" ratings to the objects with curves. Bar and Neta's theory was that the sharp and angled images conveyed a sense of threat.

DOES THE BALANCE OF THE IMAGE MATTER?

Paul Silvia and Christopher Barona (2009) wanted to see if it mattered whether the objects in an image were balanced (Figure 1.2) or unbalanced (Figure 1.3). Balanced or not, people still preferred the curved objects.

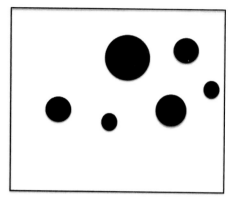 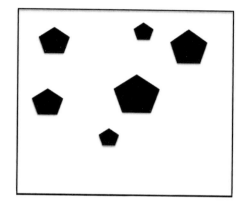

FIGURE 1.2 A balanced image.

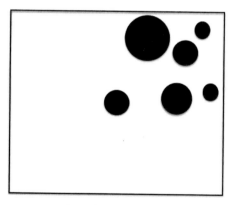 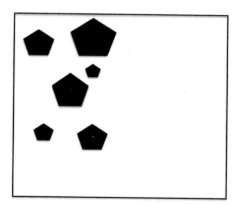

FIGURE 1.3 An unbalanced image.

What about complex shapes? Silvia and Barona tested complex, angular shapes (Figure 1.4), and complex shapes with slightly curved edges (Figure 1.5).

FIGURE 1.4 A complex, angular shape.

FIGURE 1.5 A complex shape with slightly curved edges.

Again, people preferred the objects with curves.

Helmut Leder, Pablo Tinio, and Bar (2011) asked whether this preference for curves was true for both "positive" objects (birthday cakes and teddy bears) and "negative" objects (razor blades and spiders). The results? People preferred curves in objects that were either positive or neutral, but there was *no* preference for curves in negative objects.

Note Nike, Apple, Pepsi, Coca-Cola, and dozens of other well-known brands use one or more curves in their logos, so they've obviously done their design homework.

CURVES STIMULATE THE BRAIN

Ed Connor and Neeraja Balachander took this idea into a neuroimaging lab. They used an abstract shape similar to the shape on the left in Figure 1.6, and then made a series of similar but elongated shapes like those in the rest of Figure 1.6.

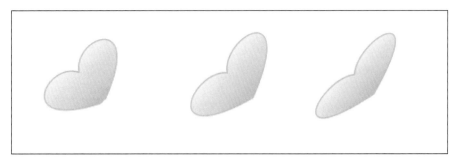

FIGURE 1.6 Curved and rounded shapes versus elongated shapes.

Not only did people prefer the softly rounded shape like the one on the left, there was more brain activity in the visual cortex when they viewed shapes that were more curved and more rounded.

Takeaways

- ☑ People prefer curves.
- ☑ When you're creating a logo, incorporate some form of curve in the design.
- ☑ When you're creating areas of color on a screen, consider using a "swoosh" or curved shape.
- ☑ When you're designing actual products—such as smartphones, remote controls, medical devices, or other hand-held items—use curved surfaces.

2 PEOPLE PREFER SYMMETRY

Whether you're choosing stock images for a web page or deciding whether to show the subject of a photo straight on or in profile, consider people's preference for symmetry.

Take any object—a photo of a face or a drawing of a circle or a seashell—and draw a line down the middle either horizontally or vertically. If the two halves on either side of the line are identical, then the object is symmetrical.

SHOW ME YOUR DNA

People rate symmetrical faces as more attractive. The theory is that this preference has to do with an evolutionary advantage of picking a mate with the best DNA.

Figures 2.1 and 2.2 show two people with different amounts of bilateral symmetry. The man in Figure 1.9 has a face that is fairly asymmetrical. The man in Figure 1.10 has a face that is more symmetrical.

FIGURE 2.1 An asymmetrical face.

FIGURE 2.2 A fairly symmetrical face.

Steven Gangestad (2010) at the University of New Mexico has researched symmetry and shown that both men and women rate people with more symmetrical features as more attractive. But symmetry isn't only about faces: bodies can be more or less symmetrical, too.

So why do people find symmetry to be more attractive? Gangestad says it may have to do with "oxidative stress." In utero, babies are exposed to free radicals that can cause DNA damage. This is called oxidative stress. The greater the oxidative stress there is, the greater the asymmetry in the face and/or body. From an evolutionary and unconscious viewpoint, people look for partners who have no DNA damage. Symmetrical features are a clue that someone has less DNA damage. As further proof, research shows that men who are rated more attractive have fewer oxidative stress chemicals in their blood.

So, when deciding what photos to use on your website, for example, choose pictures of people who are more symmetrical than less, since those people will be viewed as more attractive.

If you must use a particular person, then evaluate face and body symmetry. If the person has a symmetrical face and body, then use a photo that is shot straight on. If the person lacks facial or body symmetry, use a profile view.

 ## How is symmetry measured?

You can use a ruler and the technique described below to measure the symmetry of a face.

Note the centerline drawn down the middle of the face in Figure 2.3, and the six horizontal lines (labeled D1, D2, D3, D4, D5, and D6) drawn across it.

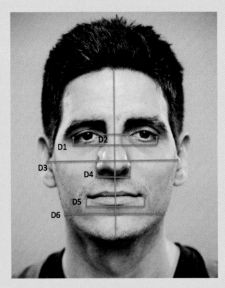

FIGURE 2.3 A face marked with symmetry lines.

Measure the distance from the left edge of D1 to the centerline.

Measure the distance from the right edge of D1 to the centerline. Write down the difference between the two lines. For example, if one side of D1 is 0.5 inches longer than the other side, write down 0.5.

Take the same measurement for D2, D3, D4, D5, and D6. It doesn't matter which side is longer or shorter. All your difference numbers should be positive—no negative numbers.

Add up all the differences.

Now do the same for Figure 2.4.

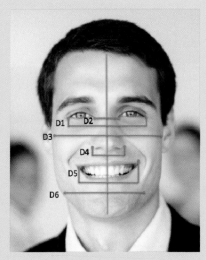

FIGURE 2.4 Another face marked with symmetry lines.

The higher the sum of the differences is, the more asymmetrical the face. If the sum of all the differences is 0, then the face is perfectly symmetrical. The further from zero the total is, the more asymmetrical the face.

IS SYMMETRY ONLY FOR MARS (FOR MEN)?

Men prefer symmetry in bodies, faces, and just about everything else, including everyday items, abstract shapes, art, and nature. But research by Kathrine Shepherd and Moshe Bar (2011) showed that women prefer symmetry in faces and bodies, but not as much as men for everything else.

If you're designing for a primarily male audience, then pay special attention to symmetry, whether it's in faces, bodies, natural or man-made objects, or product pages with TVs—try to use symmetrical objects and show them in an equal right/left and top/bottom view. Men will find symmetrical images most appealing.

If you're designing for a primarily female audience, then symmetry in faces and bodies of people is the most important. You don't have to be as concerned with making sure all the products are symmetrically displayed.

There might be an evolutionary advantage for preferring symmetry in a mate, but why do people prefer symmetry in objects? Some researchers have proposed that the brain is predisposed to look for symmetry, and so people see symmetrical objects faster and make sense of them faster. The theory is that this visual fluency with symmetrical objects makes people feel as though they prefer the objects. They may just find them easier to see and understand. But why this is true for men and not for women remains a mystery.

IS THERE ANY ADVANTAGE TO USING ASYMMETRY?

As a designer, you have to make decisions about the layout of elements on a screen or page or packaged product. Does the research on symmetry mean that your design should always be perfectly symmetrical?

Figure 2.5 shows a web page with an asymmetrical design and Figure 2.6 shows one with a more symmetrical design.

FIGURE 2.5 An asymmetrical design.

FIGURE 2.6 A fairly symmetrical design.

If you design a symmetrical layout, then you know that people will perceive it quickly and will more likely prefer it—especially if your target audience is men.

On the other hand, if you go with an asymmetrical layout, then people will most likely be surprised by it. That may grab their attention initially, but the advantage of surprise and initial attention getting may be offset by fewer people liking it.

Takeaways

☑ When you want to use pictures of people that your audience will find attractive, make sure those people have symmetrical faces and bodies.

☑ When your target audience is primarily men, use a symmetrical layout.

☑ When your target audience is primarily women, you can use a more asymmetrical layout.

3 SOME PEOPLE HAVE AN EXTRA COLOR CONE

In 1948, H. L. de Vries was studying the eyes of men who were color blind. He made an amazing discovery that he mentioned only in passing, on the last page of the paper he wrote about his research. His discovery went virtually unnoticed for more than three decades.

Before I tell you about the discovery, here's some background on color vision:

People see color with special cells in their eyes called cones. Most people have three types of cones, each of which is triggered by certain wavelengths of light. The cones send signals to the brain, and the brain interprets those signals as blue, or turquoise, or pink, or any of the other colors.

Each cone allows the eye to see approximately 100 shades, so all three cones combined result in 100 to the third power, or about 1 million, different colors that most people can see.

For some people, one or more cones don't activate in the same way—these people have one of several forms of color confusion or color blindness. They may have trouble distinguishing between certain colors, for example, red and green. People who have only two color cones working properly can see approximately 100 to the second power, or 10,000, colors. People who have only one color cone working properly can see approximately 100 colors.

Color vision is determined by the X chromosome. Men have only one X chromosome, and women have two X chromosomes. This is why more men than women are color blind.

BACK TO THE AMAZING DISCOVERY

To test the men with color blindness, de Vries had them turn dials on an instrument to mix red light and green light until they saw yellow. Because the men were color blind, they added more red or green than someone without color blindness would add.

Out of curiosity, de Vries tested the daughters of one subject and observed that even though they were not color blind—they seemed to distinguish red and green as well as anyone—they still used more red in their test light than normal people to make the match precise. If the women weren't color blind, why were they adding more red?

De Vries hypothesized that since color blindness runs in families, the mothers and daughters of the color-blind men would have four color cones, not three. They would have the three normal cones, plus the abnormal cone that the men in the family have. De Vries's idea was that having four cones enabled them to see more colors than most people, and that was why their test results were unusual. He put this idea about four cones at the end of his paper, and didn't mention it in any of his work after that.

It wasn't until the 1980s that de Vries's ideas were rediscovered by John Mollon and Gabriele Jordan, who were studying color vision in monkeys. Since color blindness is fairly common in men (9 percent of men are color blind), Mollon and Jordan realized that as many as 12 percent of the women in the world may have four cones. The name for someone who has four cones is a "tetrachromat." These women would be able to see 100 to the fourth power, or 100 million, colors.

FUNCTIONAL TETRACHROMATS ARE RARE

Much to her surprise, Jordan has had a difficult time finding women who are tetrachromats *and* can correctly do the matching tests for tetrachromacy. Why is this? It turns out that although a woman may be a tetrachromat, she may not be able to distinguish all the colors. She may report colors as though she only had three cones. The theory here is that tetrachromats are living in a world of trichromats. The objects they interact with were created by and for people who see 1 million colors, not 100 million colors, which means that tetrachromats haven't had much opportunity to learn how to distinguish between the extra colors they see.

There is some evidence to support this theory. Recently, artist Concetta Antico was tested and found to have the DNA of a tetrachromat. She also is a "functional" tetrachromat. Her early training and continued immersion in art may have taught her how to use her fourth cone.

 For more information on Concetta Antico, see the BBC story at http://www.bbc.com/future/story/20140905-the-women-with-super-human-vision.

➡ Testing for tetrachromacy

The best way to test for tetrachromacy is with a DNA test. Watch out for fake tests. In February 2015, one bogus test that went viral suggested that any viewer who could see 33 or more colors in the test image was a tetrachromat. In fact, computer displays don't display enough colors to test for tetrachromacy.

Takeaways

☑ If you're a woman with color-blind men in your family, you might be a tetrachromat. If you are, you might need special training to see the extra colors.

☑ With advances in technology, color displays are likely to show more colors in the near future. As a designer, you might be asked to—or you might want to—create designs that use the extra colors that tetrachromats can see. There might be unique designs using pictures and graphics with extra colors for those who can see them.

4 PERIPHERAL VISION DETERMINES WHERE CENTRAL VISION SHOULD LOOK

It's 11:00 a.m. on a Saturday and you're at home in front of your laptop, browsing the Internet. You open your favorite news site and scan the headlines. You click on a story and read for a bit, then go back to the main page and scan some more. You choose another story, look at the picture, and read some more—just normal scanning and reading online behavior, right?

What you may not realize as you do this is that your two types of vision, central and peripheral, are multitasking.

BUT ISN'T MULTITASKING A MYTH?

If you've read any of my other books or blog posts, you know that I'm fond of saying that multitasking doesn't exist; most of the time what people think of as multitasking is actually fast "task switching." People switch really quickly from one thing to another, from one focus to another. This quick task switching takes a toll on attention and mental processing.

But central and peripheral vision multitasking is different. People really are capable of multitasking when it comes to vision.

A QUICK DEFINITION OF CENTRAL AND PERIPHERAL VISION

The fovea is a small depression at the back of the retina that affords very clear, detailed vision. Foveal vision, or central vision, covers only a very small area—about the size of two thumbnails—but it takes up half of the processing in the brain's visual cortex.

The rest of the visual field is peripheral vision. Peripheral vision takes in a much broader and larger view. The visual cortex can process both central and peripheral vision at the same time.

EYES TAKE LOTS OF VISUAL SAMPLES AT THE SAME TIME

People take in visual information in little bites. This is called visual sampling. Central and peripheral vision are working at the same time. When you're scanning that page online and a headline grabs your attention, you move your head and your gaze so that the headline is in view of your fovea—your central vision. But how do your head and eye know to look at that exact spot?

PERIPHERAL VISION CALLS THE SHOTS

Casimir Ludwig, J. Rhys Davies, and Miguel Eckstein's research (2014) showed that it is peripheral vision—what it sees, and how that information is processed in the brain— that tells the central vision where to focus next. This is a largely unconscious process. People are consciously aware of their central vision and what it's processing, but they're likely *not* consciously aware of what's in their peripheral vision, or that their peripheral vision is calling the shots for where to look next.

TWO VISIONS ARE BETTER THAN ONE

You would think that all this multitasking would slow down visual processing, but Ludwig's research shows that central and peripheral vision are processed independently to a large extent, and, therefore, both can be done quickly.

DON'T BASE EVERY DESIGN DECISION ON EYE-TRACKING STUDIES

Most eye-tracking research measures only central vision; it doesn't address what's going on in peripheral vision. Yet there's a tendency to make design decisions based on eye-tracking results ("No one looked at this picture, therefore it's not effective and we should remove it."). Now that you know that peripheral vision is calling the shots, you can avoid making decisions based solely on eye-tracking data.

PAY ATTENTION TO PERIPHERAL VISION

Since peripheral vision directs where central vision should go, it's important to pay attention to what people will see in their peripheral vision when they focus on certain parts of a page with their central vision. Peripheral vision isn't just dead space to be left blank. As a designer, you need to design flexibly to allow for different monitor sizes and devices (large screen, laptop, tablet, smartphone). There's a tendency to use only the middle part of the screen and leave the edges blank. This might be easiest for creating one screen that translates to multiple devices, but it means that you're leaving peripheral vision with nothing to look at. Figure 4.1 shows a website for a restaurant that makes full use of peripheral vision to grab attention and help people know what the site is about.

FIGURE 4.1 A website that makes full use of peripheral vision.

Takeaways

☑ Don't base design decisions solely on eye-tracking studies.

☑ Don't leave peripheral areas blank. Instead, include information that helps people decide where to look (with central vision) next.

5 PERIPHERAL VISION SEES DANGER AND PROCESSES EMOTIONS FASTER

Think about all the things you see during a typical day. Your eyes are constantly taking in visual stimuli. But you don't *react* to everything you see. A lot of it goes by without your brain or body reacting.

Yet certain things do produce an immediate and strong reaction. If you see something that's potentially dangerous—a snake, fire, a dark shadow moving—your brain and body will react quickly.

If peripheral vision covers a bigger area than central vision, and if peripheral vision determines where you look, then it makes sense that peripheral vision is more sensitive to, and reacts faster to, images of danger than central vision. Dimitri Bayle and his team tested this idea.

A TEST OF FEARFUL FACES

Imagine walking with our ancestors, thousands of years ago, in a grassy field. If you noticed out of the corner of your eye (your peripheral vision) that the person to your left suddenly made a fearful face, that information would likely have been useful to you and perhaps would have kept you alive.

People are particularly sensitive to the emotional faces of people around them, especially if the facial expression is one of surprise or fear.

Bayle and his team researched whether people recognized facial expressions faster and more accurately than other aspects of a face, such as gender, in peripheral vision.

When the brain analyzes and interprets a face, it uses the occipital and temporal lobes, including the special part called the fusiform facial area, which is most stimulated by central vision.

If being able to recognize that someone had a fearful facial expression would keep a person alive, Bayle hypothesized that these images would go through peripheral vision, right to the amygdala via a faster and more automatic sub-cortical route, rather than through the "regular" visual areas of the occipital and temporal lobes and the fusiform facial area through central vision.

The researchers used pictures of people with expressions of fear or disgust and measured how quickly the participants identified each. They also added a gender identification task, where participants had to identify whether a neutral face (showing no emotional expression) was a face of a man or woman. This neutral gender identification task was used as a control, to compare against the fear and disgust expressions. For all of the pictures, sometimes the participants saw the pictures in peripheral vision and sometimes in central vision.

Bayle's hypotheses proved to be correct. People reacted to images of fearful expressions faster when they were shown in peripheral vision than when they were shown in central vision. They also processed disgust expressions more quickly in peripheral vision compared to central vision, but not as fast as the fear expressions. In the task where participants had to identify the gender of the image, there was no difference in reaction time between central and peripheral vision.

In addition to the faster reaction times for pictures with fear expressions, the participants could identify what they were looking at farther out in their peripheral field than with the pictures of disgust expressions or when identifying gender.

DESIGN WITH FEAR AND DANGER IN MIND

Designers usually don't intend to scare their target audience with their designs, but often they *do* want to grab viewers' attention. As mentioned earlier in this chapter, there's a tendency among designers to place very little information in viewers' peripheral vision. If you want to grab attention quickly, and *if* it's appropriate to the content and brand of what you're designing, consider using emotional or dangerous images in peripheral vision.

Takeaways

☑ To grab people's attention quickly, place images that imply danger in their peripheral vision.

☑ To grab people's attention quickly, show them pictures with strong emotional content in their peripheral vision.

---

6 PERIPHERAL VISION IS LIKE A LOW-RESOLUTION IMAGE

Let's go back to the scenario where it's 11:00 a.m. on a Saturday and you're at home in front of your laptop browsing the Internet. If I ask you what you're seeing in your central vision at any particular time, you could probably describe it fairly well. You might say, "I'm looking at text on a page. I'm reading the word 'The' and I see that the capital T is a vertical line with a shorter horizontal line on top."

But what if I asked you to describe what you're seeing in your peripheral vision while you're reading the word "The" with your central vision? It would be more difficult for you to articulate it. Your peripheral vision is blurry out toward the edges, and you're less aware of what you're seeing in peripheral vision, so it's harder to describe.

The MIT Computer Science and Artificial Intelligence Laboratory has an answer about what your peripheral vision looks like. Ruth Rosenholtz and her team have created a computer model that simulates what the brain "sees" in peripheral vision. Rosenholtz calls these simulated images "mongrels."

PERIPHERAL VISION IS BLURRY

One way to think about peripheral vision compared to central vision is that peripheral vision trades detail for an overall impression. In order to process the visual information quickly, and over a larger field than central vision, peripheral vision sends a broader view that ends up looking kind of like a really low-resolution image, and it becomes blurrier at the edges.

HOW PERIPHERAL VISION WON A DESIGN COMPETITION

In 2013, the city of Boston held a competition to redesign its mass transit map. Rosenholtz (being located at MIT in the Boston area) took the subway map as it existed before the redesign competition, and the new subway map design that won the competition, and ran both maps through her mongrel computer model.

Figure 6.1 shows the subway map before the redesign. The Kendall/MIT stop on the Red Line is circled.

Assume that your central vision is focused on that circle. According to Rosenholtz's computer model, your combined central and peripheral vision would look like Figure 6.2. The central vision area is crisp and clear, but the peripheral vision area is blurry.

FIGURE 6.1 The Boston subway transit map before the redesign.

FIGURE 6.2 The "mongrel" computer model that includes peripheral vision of the Boston subway transit map before the redesign.

Michael Kvrivishvili is a designer from Moscow who won the competition for a new map. His map is in Figure 6.3. I've placed that same circle at the Kendall stop.

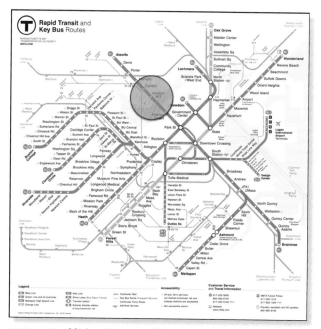

FIGURE 6.3 Michael Kvrivishvili's winning redesign. (Photo courtesy of Michael Kvrivishvili, https://www.flickr.com/photos/10247460@N03/)

Again, assuming that your central vision is focused on that circle, Figure 6.4 shows what your composite central and peripheral vision looks like with Kvrivishvili's map. It too is blurry, but there are some differences between Kvrivishvili's mongrel and the original mongrel.

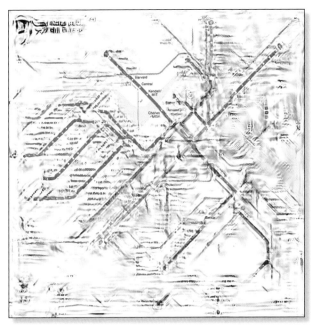

FIGURE 6.4 The "mongrel" computer model that includes peripheral vision of Kvrivishvili's winning redesign.

WHEN LESS IS MORE

In Figure 6.1, the previous version of the map, parts of the map are geographically correct, for example, the western part of the Green Line and the southern part of the Red Line. But they are also fairly complex, so in the Figure 6.2 mongrel model, these features of the map lose informational impact.

Compare those areas to Kvrivishvili's redesigned map in Figure 6.3. His map is less literal, and more representational. In Figure 6.4, peripheral vision is able to keep the gist of those areas truer to the information they are attempting to convey, even if the visual design is less correct geographically. By simplifying the design, Kvrivishvili increases clarity, especially when it comes to peripheral vision.

DESIGNING FOR BOTH VISION STATES

Probably without realizing it, many designers design primarily for central vision. After all, central vision is the vision designers are most familiar with and most conscious of. But you may want to design for peripheral vision as well. Try to simplify the design, especially on the outer edges.

Assuming you don't have Rosenholtz's mongrel computer model, you can try a simple peripheral vision test of your own. Pick a part of your design that you expect people to be looking at with central vision, for example, a navigation bar at a website, and then, while keeping your central vision there, see if you can get an impression of the rest of the screen. Does it need to be simplified to convey information through the peripheral vision channel?

A SURPRISING GUIDELINE FOR DESIGNING FOR SCREEN SIZE

One of the interesting conclusions from this research on peripheral vision goes against some oft-repeated design wisdom. It's common to find guidelines that say, for example, that icons and logos on a smartphone should be both smaller and simpler than those on a desktop. On the surface, this makes sense: if the icons or logos are highly detailed, they'll become muddier and harder to perceive as the screen gets smaller.

However, there's another way to think about this interplay of size and visual detail. On a large screen, a small percentage of the visual area is within central vision. Most of the screen is in peripheral vision. On a smaller screen, the amount of the screen within central vision increases compared to the amount of the screen within peripheral vision. These days smartphones are getting bigger. With a large smartphone, it's certainly possible to have both central and peripheral vision active, but even then as much as 75 percent of the visual field will be in central vision. On a relatively small smartphone screen, most or all of the visual field may be within central vision. And with a small device, such as a smartwatch, chances are that the entire display is within central vision.

The more of the visual field that's in central vision, the more detail you can use, not less. Central vision will pick up the detail. As the screen gets larger, a logo at the top left, or an icon at the top right is likely appearing in peripheral vision, which means that the logo or icon should be *simpler,* so that peripheral vision will have an easier time picking it up visually and understanding what it is—the opposite of some of some current design guidelines.

Takeaways

☑ Whether you're designing a stand-alone image, an infographic, or a web page, design for both peripheral and central vision.

☑ Since peripheral vision is blurry, make the design in the outer edges simple.

☑ When you're designing a small display (for example, a smartphone), the design can be more detailed.

☑ When you're designing for a larger display (for example, a laptop), the design should be simpler and less detailed.

7 EMOTION VS. GAZE DIRECTION: EMOTION WINS

Imagine you're looking at a screen showing a picture of a person looking at a product, like the picture shown in Figure 7.1.

FIGURE 7.1 An image of a person looking at a product.

Will your gaze go to the same place as the gaze of the person in the picture? The answer is yes.

But there's more to this than there may first appear to be.

THE INFLUENCE OF GAZE DIRECTION

Anecdotal evidence shows that people will follow the gaze of a person in a photo. Most of this evidence is based on heat map and/or eye tracking data.

There *is* a peer-reviewed study by Giovanni Galfano (2012) that backs up the gaze direction claims, but the research has an interesting add-on result. Galfano and his team told participants that they would see a shape appear on a screen, on either the left or right. When the shape appeared, the participants were supposed to press the space bar as quickly as possible.

In some of the trials, the participants would simply see the shape and press the space bar. But in others, two things would happen before the target shape appeared. First, the word "left" or "right" (in Italian, as this study was conducted in Italy) would appear in the middle of the screen. The word was always an accurate clue as to where the target shape would appear. But between the display of the word and the display of the target shape, another clue would display. This was a cartoon face in the middle of the screen, looking either left or right. Sometimes the face gave a correct clue; sometimes the face looked to the right, but the target shape appeared on the left, or vice versa. The words were always accurate, but the cartoon's gaze was not always accurate.

In a second version of the study, an arrow pointed to the left or right instead of a cartoon face gazing to the left or right.

The participants were told to pay attention to the words "left" and "right" and to ignore the faces and arrows. Of course they couldn't ignore them. When the faces or the arrows appeared and looked in the wrong direction from where the target shape showed up, the participants took more time to press the space bar. The participants were trying to, but couldn't, ignore the face or the arrows.

So isn't this evidence that we look in the direction that either a face is gazing or an arrow is pointing? Well, yes, but...

IS LOOKING THE SAME AS TAKING ACTION?

Galfano suggests that if you're designing an ad, a product page, or a landing page, you could use a picture of person, a cartoon face, or an arrow all gazing or pointing in a certain direction. And now you know that any of those cues will increase the likelihood that visitors will look there too. But will they take action? Will they press a button? Will they fill in a form? Sometimes you want people to do more than look in a particular direction. You want them to take an action, press a button, or click on a link. Is gaze the best way to do that?

Scientific research is slim on this question, but Jon Correll from Conversion Voodoo (www.conversionvoodoo.com) did some A/B testing that lays out a model for testing what gets people to take action. (For any graduate students who are reading this, this would be a great thesis for a peer-reviewed journal.)

Correll's hypothesis was that conveying emotion is more effective in getting people to take action than having the viewer look in a certain direction. Correll did a series of landing page tests. He kept the landing page the same for each test and changed only the picture of the person. He did the test with over 150,000 unique visitors, and tested ten different images. Each image was of the same model, wearing the same color (white), but it varied in the direction she was facing, her use of arms and pointing, and her facial expression. Sometimes she looked at the call to action, but other times she looked directly at the viewer. Sometimes she pointed to the call to action, but sometimes she didn't. In every picture, the model looks happy, but in some she looks much more animated and excited than others.

Figure 7.2 shows Correll's baseline image. He measured the percentage of visitors who pressed on the call to action of the landing page with this image—where the model is looking at and gesturing toward the call to action—and then compared that to all the other images.

Figure 7.3 shows the other images that were tested. The percentage on each image displays how much better or worse each image was in getting visitors to click in comparison to the baseline image. Images with red numbers did worse than the baseline. Images with yellow numbers did somewhat better than the baseline. And images with green numbers did much better than the baseline.

FIGURE 7.2 Jon Correll's baseline image (Research by Jon Corell).

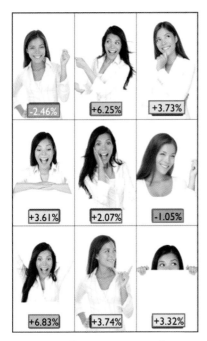

FIGURE 7.3 The gaze images that were tested.

These results are not conclusive, but there's a trend. Pointing is better than not pointing. Gazing is better than just looking straight ahead. But there's one critical caveat: high emotion seems to be best of all.

Takeaways

- ☑ When you want people to look at a particular place on a screen or page, put a picture of someone who looks really excited next to the part of the page where you want people to look.

- ☑ Although it's true that people will look where a face is looking, when you use a face that's displaying a lot of emotion, people are more inclined to take action.

- ☑ If you don't want to use a picture of a person gazing at a certain spot, you can use an arrow pointing to where you want your audience to look. An arrow is just as effective as a gazing face, but neither is as effective as a face displaying positive, excited emotion.

8 DIRECT GAZE CAN BACKFIRE

If you've ever worked with a coach to improve your ability to communicate persuasively, you probably learned how important it is to look directly at people when you're talking to them. The rule of thumb is that looking at someone directly when you're speaking makes you appear confident. It makes your message more persuasive.

It turns out that, in some situations, direct gaze can backfire and actually be *less* persuasive.

Frances Chen (2013) and her team put this idea to the test using videos of people speaking. In a series of studies, participants watched videos of people talking about controversial political topics. Here's what Chen found:

- If participants agreed with the speaker's message, then they spontaneously looked at the speaker's eyes.

- If participants disagreed with the speaker's message, then they tended *not* to look at the speaker's eyes.

- If the speaker was angled slightly away and did not maintain eye contact with the camera, then participants were more likely to be persuaded by the speaker and change their opinion.

- If participants were told to watch the speaker's eyes and the participants did not agree with the speaker, then they did *not* change their opinion on the topic.

- If participants were told to watch the speaker's mouth rather than their eyes, then the participants were more likely to be persuaded to change their opinion.

In her discussion of the research, Chen refers to the idea that direct gaze is used in two different ways. One is "affiliative." People look directly at the speaker when they're being social, when they want to engage with the speaker, and when they're open to affiliation or agreement with the speaker.

But another way that people use direct gaze is to intimidate. If people don't agree with what the speaker is saying and if the speaker is looking right at them, the gaze will seem more confrontational than affiliative. If the gaze is confrontational, then people will be on guard and defensive, and the gaze will not be persuasive.

Designers often have to make decisions about whether to use a photo that involves direct gaze. Video producers have to make decisions about whether to shoot promotional videos with someone speaking directly into the camera or off to the side. The answer based on the research is "it depends." It depends on whether the message is controversial, and whether the people watching the video are most likely already in agreement with the speaker, or if the speaker is trying to persuade them.

Use the flowchart in Figure 8.1 to help you decide whether or not to use an image or speaker with direct gaze.

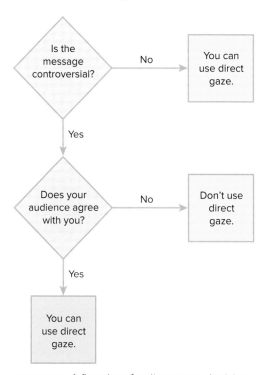

FIGURE 8.1 A flowchart for direct gaze decision.

Takeaways

- ☑ When your target audience might not agree with the message, use an image of an individual who is gazing slightly off to the side.
- ☑ When your target audience agrees with your message, you can use direct gaze.
- ☑ When the purpose of your message is to connect in a social way (and not to persuade) and when the message is not controversial, you can use direct gaze.

9 PEOPLE DECIDE ABOUT A DESIGN IN A SPLIT SECOND

It's ironic. You spend hours, days, weeks, or even months working on the visual design of an infographic or a website. Yet research by Katharina Reinecke, Lane Harrison, and the team at the University of Michigan shows that people make lasting judgments about the design's appeal in 500 ms (one-half of a second) or less.

According to their research, this first impression sticks and influences later opinions about the usability and trustworthiness of the website or product.

Reinecke (2013) and her team started by collecting web pages in various languages. They selected 450 websites, with a range of visual complexity and use of color. They analyzed each page on a variety of metrics, such as hue, saturation, color intensity, symmetry, balance, and equilibrium.

Next they validated these metrics by showing the websites to the participants for 500 ms, and had the participants rate them: 184 people rated 30 websites for visual complexity, and 122 rated 30 websites for colorfulness. (They tested all 450 websites, but each person rated only 30.)

Now the team had 450 websites with validated metrics. The last part of the study was to show the websites for 500 ms to a new group of people. Instead of rating for complexity or colorfulness, however, these people rated the websites on visual appeal. The team tested 242 people in this phase of the experiment.

So what were the results for the visual appeal ratings of websites?

- Visual complexity was the most important factor in a website being rated as visually appealing. Most appealing were websites of low to medium visual complexity. High visual complexity resulted in the lowest visual appeal scores.

- Participants older than 45 liked websites with a low visual complexity more than the other age groups.

- Participants with a PhD didn't like websites that were highly colorful; the same was true of those with only a high school diploma.

- There were no significant differences between men and women.

TESTING INFOGRAPHICS INSTEAD OF WEBSITES

Harrison, Reinecke, and Remco Chang (2015) used the same methodology to test 330 infographics for visual appeal. They had 1,278 participants rate infographics after viewing them for 500 ms.

The results for the infographics visual appeal ratings were as follows:

- There was a lot of variability in the infographic ratings. Only a few of the 330 infographics were universally appealing. Unlike the website research, infographics that some people rated very highly were rated very low by others.

- As with the websites, colorfulness and visual complexity were the important variables when it came to judging a design as visually appealing. However, with the infographics, colorfulness was more important than visual complexity—the opposite result of the website ratings.

- Looking at the data overall, infographics that were colorful were rated as more appealing. However, there's an important effect hidden in the color data: men didn't like the colorful infographics, and women did.

- There were also gender effects for complexity. Visual complexity didn't affect men's ratings of visual appeal, but women tended to like infographics that were less complex.

- Most people did not like infographics with a lot of text, but women were more affected by this than men. The amount of text was not a strong influence for men, but the women preferred infographics with more images.

- Education had a small effect. The more education a person had, the more they preferred less colorful and less complex infographics. But gender was a stronger effect than education.

DESIGNING FOR AN AUDIENCE

It's probably not news to you that not everyone reacts to visual design in the same way. But sometimes designers unconsciously start designing what they think works well, rather than taking the target audience into account.

Depending on what you're designing, and whom you're designing for, you may want to consider changing the complexity, the amount of color, or even the amount of text. Be careful of using your aesthetic when making these decisions. You may not be representative of your target audience.

Takeaways

- ☑ People tend to make quick and lasting decisions about design, so make sure your design has quick and unconscious visual appeal.

- ☑ When designing a website, don't underestimate the importance of visual complexity. Research shows visual complexity is the most important variable people use in deciding how visually appealing your site is, and gender doesn't matter when it comes to visual complexity and website design.

- ☑ When designing a website, use low to medium visual complexity for maximum appeal.

- ☑ When your target audience is mainly people over age 45, reduce the visual complexity of the design.

- ☑ When you're designing an infographic and your target audience is primarily men, use less color.

- ☑ When you're designing an infographic and your target audience is primarily women, reduce the visual complexity and use less text.

HOW PEOPLE THINK AND REMEMBER

Some people say that humans are irrational and illogical. Logic and rationality are not the brain's normal mode. This chapter looks at how people usually think and examines some of the newest research on how memories are formed and retrieved.

10 PEOPLE USE TWO KINDS OF THINKING

Try for 30 seconds to multiply these two numbers in your head, not using pen and paper or a calculator:

17 x 24

It's difficult to do in your head—most people I ask this of give up in a few minutes. It's just too hard.

Here's another task. Look at the photo in Figure 10.1 and decide what it's a photo of.

FIGURE 10.1 What is this a photo of?

Most people say it's a picture of a little boy who is sad.

Why did I ask you these questions?

SYSTEM 1 AND SYSTEM 2 THINKING

Those two experiences—doing a multiplication problem in your head, and identifying the photo as a picture of a sad boy, feel very different. According to Daniel Kahneman, author of *Thinking, Fast and Slow* (2013), these are examples of the difference between System 1 and System 2 thinking.

When you looked at the photo of the little boy, and decided what it was, that was a quick and easy task. You didn't have to think hard about it. That's an example of System 1 thinking. System 1 thinking, Kahneman says, is quick, intuitive, easy, and effortless.

System 2 thinking is different. When you had to multiply the two numbers in your head, that was an example of System 2 thinking. System 2 thinking is difficult. It takes a lot of effort.

Note You can tell when people are doing System 2 (hard, effortful) thinking because their pupils dilate while they're doing it.

SYSTEM 1 IS THE NORMAL MODE

Kahneman asserts in his book that System 1 thinking (quick, intuitive, easy thinking) is people's natural or normal mode. Most of the time, most people are in System 1 mode.

System 2 thinking is activated only when people encounter something difficult to do (like multiplication in their heads). When that happens, System 1 gives up very quickly and turns to System 2 to take over.

Because people do System 1 thinking most of the time, they actually can make some interesting mistakes in their thought process.

The chapter on Reading explores how fonts interact with System 1 and System 2 thinking in unexpected ways. And the chapter on How People Shop and Buy explains how System 1 thinking influences pricing and how many items people buy.

THE OPPOSITE OF "DON'T MAKE ME THINK"

In his great book, *Don't Make Me Think*, Steve Krug says that for a product to be usable, it needs to be easy to use so people don't have to think. And it's true that easy to use equals less thinking.

But, there's another side to consider: If you want people to think carefully about something before they take action on it, then you need to have them do something difficult first to kick them out of System 1 mode and into System 2. Otherwise they're likely to make errors.

As a designer, you probably don't try to make people think harder by giving them something difficult to do, but if it's important that people carefully think something through, then you may want to make them think. For example, if someone is landing a plane, doing surgery, or operating a nuclear power plant, you may want her to be in System 2 mode for at least part of the task.

You can kick people out of System 1 mode and into System 2 mode fairly easily. Here are some examples of ways to do that:

- Show them text in a font that is moderately hard to read, for example:

  Because this text looks like script and because there isn't much contrast between the text and the background, it is harder to read.

- Give them a moderately hard math problem to do without any external aids, like the multiplication at the beginning of this chapter.

- Ask them to solve a word problem, such as:

  A bat and a ball cost $1.10 in total. The bat costs $1 more than the ball. How much does the ball cost?

The System 1 answer is that the ball costs $0.10 ($1.00 for the bat and another $0.10 for the ball). But if the bat costs $1.00 *more* than the ball, and if the ball is $0.10, then the bat would be $1.10 and the total would be $1.20. So the correct answer is that the ball costs $0.05 and the bat is $1.05, for a total of $1.10.

- Here's another one:

  If it takes 5 machines 5 minutes to make 5 widgets, how long would it take 100 machines to make 100 widgets?

The System 1 answer is that it would take 100 minutes. But if you analyze the problem from a System 2 mode, if 5 machines make 5 widgets in 5 minutes, then it's taking just 5 minutes to make the widgets. So if you had 100 machines making 100 widgets, it would still just take 5 minutes.

System 1 mode makes a lot of errors like this. If you want people to think carefully about something and not make these errors, you have to get them to switch to System 2 mode. You do that by making them think hard.

DESIGN FOR ERRORS

When you're working on a product, you're usually immersed in the design. This means that you're not looking at the product from the point of view of someone who is seeing or using it for the first time, or someone who hasn't seen it or used it for three months. You know how everything works. The user doesn't.

It's easy in the design phase to underestimate how many errors people will make. They won't find the Control button. They won't remember where a link is located. They won't remember what a label means.

This is exacerbated by System 1 thinking. People are just not thinking that hard. Assume they aren't, and assume they'll be making lots of mistakes. Your job then, as a designer, is to make sure that it's easy to recover from mistakes.

Takeaways

☑ Since most people use System 1 thinking most of the time, assume that they'll make errors. Give them good feedback when they make mistakes and let them undo or easily change what they've done.

☑ When you want people to think about something carefully, give them something difficult to do first, so they switch to System 2 thinking. Ask a difficult question or use a harder to read font so that System 2 will kick in.

11 SOME MEMORIES CHANGE EASILY

Think back to when you were last at a family gathering or an annual work celebration. You run the event back in your mind, and it almost seems like you're watching a movie. People tend to think that memories like this are stored in their brains like digital recordings of specific facts or events. But that's not how memories are stored or retrieved.

The latest research on memory shows that memories are formed from particular neurons firing. Your brain is being rewired every time you form a memory. But your brain is also firing when you retrieve the memory. And every time you retrieve the memory, it may change based on new information and new memories. You re-create the memory when you retrieve it, so it's subject to new neuron firings. Each time you retrieve the memory it changes a little more, especially for this type of memory.

AUTOBIOGRAPHICAL MEMORIES

People talk about memory as though all memories are the same, but there are actually many different kinds of memory. The example of the family reunion is an autobiographical memory. Autobiographical memories have to do with a specific event in your own life. These memories are subject to errors because they are re-created each time you bring them to consciousness from memory. Anything that's occurred since you first created the memory may affect the original memory. For example, say you remember that your Aunt Kathy was at the family reunion last August, but actually she wasn't at that reunion, she was at the holiday party in October. The memory has been altered and you probably aren't aware of the alteration.

When people use your website to order clothes, you may not realize it, but they're creating autobiographical memories. This means that how they remember the experience of using the website may not be accurate.

At the end of user testing of a product, I often ask people to talk about what they were thinking and what they experienced. It's only been an hour or less, but even after that amount of time the memories of the experience are often different than the experience itself.

During a user test of a clothing website, one participant commented that he didn't like the purple colors at the website. Half an hour later, when we were discussing his experience, he commented on how much he liked the colors at the website. Another person I tested using online banking software to send a wire transfer was so frustrated that she alternated between using bad language and being almost in tears. Half an hour later she said she thought the site was really easy to use. I told her she didn't have to say that,

that she could be honest about her experience. She looked at me in confusion and said, "I am being honest."

STRONG EMOTIONS MAKE STRONG MEMORIES

Another type of autobiographical memory is called a flashbulb memory. This kind of memory has a very strong emotional charge. If I ask you what you were doing on July 21, 2008, you probably won't remember much, and your memories may be vague, "Was that a weekday? If it was a weekday, I was probably at work."

However, if I ask you what you were doing when you found out about the attack on the World Trade Center in New York City on September 11, 2001, you probably have a very strong memory of where you were and what you were doing, because that memory was encoded with a strong emotional charge.

TEN YEARS LATER

Within a week of September 11, 2001, several researchers joined together (William Hirst, 2015) in the US and sent out surveys about the event. They then sent out follow-up surveys to the same people 11 months, 25 months, and 119 months (almost 10 years) after the event.

They found that people's memories of the event (where they were, how they reacted, what happened during the event) changed a lot in the first year, and included many inaccuracies. After the first year the memories stabilized—meaning they didn't change, but they still contained many inaccuracies. So far, at the 10-year mark the memories remain stable, but still inaccurate.

The researchers also studied whether external events—how much people watched media accounts, talked to friends, or were personally affected by the events, for example—had an effect on the memories or their inaccuracies. They found no effect.

Most autobiographical memories activate the hippocampus in the brain. Flashbulb memories also activate the amygdala, which is where emotions are processed. Like autobiographical memories, flashbulb memories change a lot. People's 9/11 memories are susceptible to alteration from news reports, and conversations with family and friends about that day. They're a little different than alterations in regular autobiographical memories. Regular autobiographical memories continue to change over time. Flashbulb memories change a lot over about a year and then seem to resist change after that.

CAN MEMORIES BE ERASED?

Did you see the movie *Eternal Sunshine of the Spotless Mind* that came out a few years ago? It's about a service people can hire to erase specific memories. When the movie came out there was speculation that this might be possible, but strong proof wasn't in. Now, however, we know that it *is* possible to erase memories.

In fact, there are several ways to erase a memory. They're all based on the idea that when you retrieve a memory you're actually not retrieving an intact memory and playing it back—you're re-creating the nerve impulses and brain activity you had when you first formed the memory. If you can disrupt the nerve firings, then you can't create the memory—ever.

There are several ways to disrupt the firings:

1. Particular proteins facilitate the process of forming a memory. If those proteins are stopped from being created, then you won't form a memory. There are drugs that inhibit the protein.

2. Xenon gas interferes with signal pathways in the brain, so if you breathe xenon gas while recalling a memory, it will erase the memory. Xenon gas is used as an anesthetic.

3. Laser light can change genes and, in doing so, change a memory. The laser light turns genes on or off by stimulating or inhibiting proteins. Interestingly, this method of memory erasing, called optogenetics, is reversible. Amy Chuong (2014) now has developed a way of doing this that doesn't require a brain implant. It can all be done with light outside the brain.

Takeaways

☑ Because memory is easily changed, you can't rely on what people say they were thinking or feeling while using a product. You have to observe what they do.

☑ When you're conducting user testing or feedback sessions with the target audience on your product, make a video recording of the testing or interview sessions since *your* memory will also be faulty.

12 REPETITION STRENGTHENS SOME MEMORIES

Autobiographical and flashbulb memories are subject to change, but other kinds of memories resist change if they're repeated enough.

MEMORIZING FACTS

Semantic memory is memory of facts. "Is Paris the capital of France?" is a question that uses semantic memory. So is "What is 9 x 6?" Once semantic memory is set, it's not subject to as many changes as autobiographical or flashbulb memories. The tricky thing about semantic memory is not retrieving it once it's set, but getting it to set—the psychologist's term is "encode." While people are learning these facts, they're subject to change and retrieval errors because the neuron firing traces aren't very strong. But when they repeat the fact over and over, the neuron trace gets stronger and is less likely to change. It's possible to make someone believe (incorrectly) that Lyon is the capital of France, but you'd have to repeat that a lot for it to begin to replace Paris in memory once she's learned Paris.

LEARNING MOTOR SKILLS

Another type of memory that stays constant is called procedural or muscle memory. When you learn how to drive a car, ride a bike, or type on a keyboard, you're using muscle memory. This type of memory also requires a lot of repetition to be set, but once set, it's hard to change or forget. Once you learn to ride a bicycle, you'll be able to ride a bicycle forever, even if you don't ride one for a while. If you haven't been on a bike for 20 years, the first minute or two might be a little rocky, but then the muscle memory for this skill is activated and the memory returns intact. This is why it's so important to learn a motor task correctly the first time. If someone learns to use two fingers to type on a keyboard rather than using the standard two hands on the home row, it will be hard for her to unlearn that and learn how to type keeping all her fingers on the home row.

SENSORY MEMORY

Memories of senses—vision, touch, hearing, smell, and taste—are stored for different amounts of time. As you're reading this book, your visual sensory memory (iconic memory) is activated for a few seconds. Your brain is remembering the letters you're seeing just long enough to string a few words together. Your brain remembers the sounds you hear (echoic memory) long enough to make sense of a particular sentence. The same is true of touch, but taste and smell are different. When you smell something (olfactory sense) and taste something (since smell is so active in taste), the sense impression bypasses most of the higher brain, where vision and sound are processed, and goes straight to the amygdala, where emotions are processed. Smell and taste memories are not easily changed. And because the amygdala is involved, a smell or taste may elicit a strong emotional reaction and a memory.

DESIGN AND SEMANTIC, MUSCLE, AND SENSORY MEMORY

So, what's the relationship between design and these kinds of memory?

You may not realize that when people interact with software, an app, a website, or a product, they're encoding and retrieving semantic, sensory, and muscle memory almost constantly. You think they're focused on the task that your product allows them to do—paying bills with the online banking app you designed, editing a movie with the editing software you designed, or choosing what to watch with the remote control you designed. And they'd agree with you. They think they're doing tasks with the product, too. Of course they are, but in the background, much of what they're really doing is retrieving semantic, muscle, and sensory memories. If you're designing anything for people to use, then you're actually designing the retrieval of memory traces.

Because I use my smartphone a lot and because I can set it up the way I want it, I have semantic, sensory, and muscle memory of how to look at the weather forecast, check my email, or connect with my friends on Facebook.

When I wake up in the morning, I reach for my phone. I'm not even out of bed. I'm not even awake. I grab the phone, click the button that brings the screen to life, and touch the icon for email. I use:

- Touch sensory memory combined with muscle memory to know that I have to physically click the round button (not just touch it) and to know where it's located. I can find that button without vision.

- Semantic memory to remember what I usually check (weather, email, Facebook)

- Visual sensory memory to move to the part of the screen where I know certain icons will be and to recognize the icons, and muscle memory to start moving my finger or thumb to the place on the screen even while my visual sensory memory is remembering where to go

- Echoic sensory memory to respond in a certain way when I hear an audio alert, ping, bell, or chime

  And so on.

Let's look at an online banking app. I use a banking app from a large US financial organization. Seventy percent of the time I use it to deposit a check, 20 percent of the time I use it to transfer money from one account to another, and 10 percent of the time I'm checking balances. Yet when I log on to the banking app from my phone, depositing a check and transferring money are hidden in the Menu icon. And the Menu icon moves. Sometimes it's at the top and sometimes it's at the bottom; sometimes it's on the left and sometimes on the right. This means I have to use my semantic memory to remember that these functions are hidden in the menu, and then my sensory and muscle memory to get there.

The same is true of desktop applications. If I'm editing a video, I have a lot of semantic memory demands. For example, transitions between frames are categorized as wipes, movements, or blurs. The transition I like to use is stored in semantic memory. My muscle memory helps me scroll to the part of the timeline I want and, as I get more adept, muscle memory lets me use the mouse to move sliders. Sensory memory helps me identify whether what I'm looking at on the screen is a project or library (based on the icon).

When you design, if you know what people want to do the most, then you can design the product to make those things easy to encode and retrieve with these types of memories. You can put things in the same place, use icons that are familiar and standard, and use semantic cues that people have seen before.

Note You may have heard that you should play brain games to improve your memory. Kirk Ericsson (2014) showed that getting physical exercise does more for your memory than brain games.

Takeaways

☑ Decide what tasks are the most frequent and important that people will be doing with your product. Then base your design decisions about icons, buttons, naming, categorization, and location on these frequent and important actions.

☑ Be as consistent as possible with design decisions. When there are industry standards for buttons, links, naming conventions, or icons, use them. It's one less thing your audience has to encode.

13 MUSIC EVOKES MEMORIES AND MOODS

We've all had the experience of hearing a song and being transported in memory to some time in the past.

Research on music and memory shows that certain songs (or even words to a song) stimulate neuron firings of certain memory traces. Music activates more areas in the brain than any other sensory stimulus.

The effect is so strong that it's now a therapy for people with dementia. When music from their past is played to them, they not only enjoy it, but it also stimulates lucidity and memories.

Note For more information on music, memories, and dementia, watch this clip from the documentary Alive Inside: https://www.youtube.com/watch?t=376&v=fyZQf0p73QM

Note Elizabeth Margulis (2013), director of the Music Cognition Lab at the University of Arkansas, showed that the emotional parts of the brain are more active when people listen to familiar music, even if they don't like it.

MUSIC AND MOOD

Listening to music can change people's mood, sometimes in a matter of seconds. Adding music to a video, ad, movie, or TV program can change the emotional impact of the piece, and change people's behavior.

If you want to move people to action, consider adding music to your message.

Note Mona Lisa Chanda (2013) reviewed 400 studies and concluded that music stimulates the immune system and, in some situations, is more effective than anti-anxiety medication.

PEOPLE RESPOND IN A SIMILAR WAY

Daniel Abrams (2013) found that brain activity was synced among people who were listening to the same music. He also saw brain activity in areas that control movement, attention, planning, and memory, even when people were sitting still listening to music.

Note Björn Vickhoff (2013) studied the heart rates of people singing together in a choir. Everyone's heart rate started synchronizing when they sang together. A slow, structured beat had the biggest effect, and also slowed down everyone's heartbeat.

Takeaways

☑ Whether you're designing a video, ad, public space, or website, you can use music to grab attention and to set a mood.

☑ When you want to stimulate memory, you may need to choose music that's specific to a given person (or let the person choose her own music). But when you just want to grab attention or improve mood, you don't have to use familiar or individualized music.

☑ Test your music with your target audience. If they like the music, you can assume that most people will react in a similar way.

HOW
PEOPLE
DECIDE

Whether or not you intend for people to make decisions as they interact with your designs, they *will* be making decisions. Because people make decisions constantly: little ones, big ones, simple ones, complex ones. Research in psychology shows that most of these decisions are made unconsciously. Neuroscientists can now look into the brain and see how and where and when and why decisions are made. The results coming out of this new field may surprise you.

14 PEOPLE MAKE DECISIONS WITH SYSTEM 1 (TRUTHINESS) THINKING

In October 2005, Stephen Colbert, an American political satirist, used the term "truthiness" during the pilot of his program *The Colbert Report*.

Colbert described truthiness as knowing in your gut that something is true as opposed to knowing through facts, logic, or evidence. The word "truthiness" caught on—you can now find entries for it in online reference sites, like this one at Dictionary.com:

> The quality of seeming to be true according to one's intuition, opinion, or perception without regard to logic, factual evidence, or the like.

Note The Merriam-Webster dictionary named "truthiness" the word of the year in 2006, but Colbert didn't actually invent the word. As pointed out by Benjamin Zimmer, a linguist, "truthiness" appears in the Oxford English Dictionary as a form of the word "truthy"; it means truthfulness. This means that Colbert was using the word "truthiness" in a truly truthy way.

Research shows that people *do* believe information that they feel is correct "from their gut," and that truthiness is the way many people remember events and make decisions.

If I asked you "Is China a country in Asia?," you would probably be able to quickly and correctly answer this question by relying on your knowledge and your memory. But there are other similar questions I could ask you that you wouldn't be as sure about. For example, if I asked you "Is there a Gutenberg printing press museum in Mainz, Germany?," you might only be able to answer correctly if you'd read books about Gutenberg, or traveled to Mainz. (The answer, by the way, is yes.)

Most of the time people are in System 1 thinking mode. System 1 is intuitive and quick. System 1 relies on Colbert's "truthiness." This means that you may try to answer the question about the Gutenberg museum based on gut alone.

Sometimes, and maybe even a lot of the time, these intuitive truthiness decisions can be correct. But sometimes they're not. And these gut decisions are easily influenced.

REPETITION MAKES PEOPLE TRUST THEIR GUT

What influences people when they're deciding whether or not something is true? Research on this question goes back at least as far as the late 1970s. In 1977, Lynn Hasher's research showed that if people hear false information enough times, then they come to believe that it's true. The theory is that repetition makes the information seem easier to recall. This feeling of easy cognitive processing combines with the feeling of familiarity. System 1 senses when something is familiar and easy to understand and then decides that it's trustworthy and true.

If you're in charge of a website or email campaign, make sure you repeat information several times and in several places. As the source of the content, you may forget how often you have to repeat things. That's because you're very familiar with the information. It's easy to forget that other people, such as your target audience, aren't as familiar. To you, it may seem that you're saying the same things over and over, but that repetition is critical if you want the information to stick with your target audience.

PHOTO + INFORMATION = TRUTHINESS

You probably already know that combining a photo with text—for example, showing a picture with a recipe—provides context and makes textual information easy to understand. But you may not realize that a photo can also increase people's tendency to believe information, even when it's not true.

Steven Frenda (2013) showed photos with news clips for political events that had occurred over the previous ten years. Some of the photos and news clips were real, and some had been altered so that they looked real, but described events that had not happened.

For example, one fake story included a photo of President Obama shaking hands with former Iranian President Mahmoud Ahmadinejad with this text:

> "April 20, 2009: President Obama, greeting heads of state at a United Nations conference, shakes the hand of Iranian President Mahmoud Ahmadinejad. White House aides say the encounter was unplanned and the handshake was a formality."

Another fake story included a picture of President George W. Bush at the wheel of a pickup truck with Roger Clemens with this text:

> "September 1, 2005: As parts of New Orleans lie underwater in the wake of Hurricane Katrina, President Bush entertains Houston Astros pitcher Roger Clemens at his ranch in Crawford, Texas."

After participants viewed each photo and news clip they chose from these four options:

1. I remember seeing this.

2. I don't remember seeing it, but I remember it happening.

3. I don't remember it.

4. I have a different memory of how it happened.

They could also respond to the following free-form questions:

- How did you feel about [this event] at the time?

- Looking back, how do you feel about it today?

Frenda tested 2,650 participants. At the beginning of the study, participants saw three true events. This was to see how much people remembered these types of events at all. Most of the participants (82 percent) chose either "I remember seeing it" or "I remember it happening" for each of the true events. And almost everyone (98 percent) remembered seeing at least two of the three events.

Then the participants viewed one of five fake events and photos. Half of the 2,650 participants reported that they remembered the false event, and of those that reported remembering the event, half of those (or 27 percent of the total participants) said that they not only remembered the event, but also remembered seeing it on the news at the time. Only 6 percent of the participants said that they remembered it differently. The rest (44 percent) said that they didn't remember the event.

Some participants even commented about their reaction to the event when it occurred. For example, for one of the fake photos about an event during Hillary Clinton's campaigning for the Democratic nomination in 2008, one participant wrote in the free-form question area:

> "I thought it was a desparate [sic] move and it solidified my disgust with Mrs. Clinton as a candidate."

Note In a second study, the researchers found that political affiliation affected false memories. Liberals tended to think that false reports that made conservatives look bad were true, and conservatives tended to think that false reports that made liberals look bad were true.

I'm not advocating that you use doctored photos and fake information to falsely affect people's memories. In fact, knowing about this research means that you have to make sure that false photos and information aren't intentionally or accidentally communicated. It's all too easy for false information to end up online and then be repeated everywhere, combining the photo/information effect with the repetition effect! You may want to assign a member of your team to be the fact-checker for your websites and other information products to make sure you're not adding to this problem.

The influence of photos on the decision of truthiness holds even when evaluating factual information. Erin Newman (2015) paired photos with the statement "Macadamia nuts are in the same evolutionary family as peaches." Sometimes the photo would be related to the text, for example, a photo of a bowl containing macadamia nuts.

Sometimes the photo would have nothing to do with the topic, and sometimes there was no photo at all.

If there was a related photo, then people were more likely to rate the statement as true.

Note Newman found that the truthiness effect could last a long time, with people believing the information for days, months, or longer if there was a related photo.

Newman's hypothesis was that a photo speeds up processing and decision making and adds to the feeling of easy cognitive processing and familiarity. Here's the set of equations:

Photo = easy to understand

and

Easy to understand = familiar

so

Familiar = true

People aren't aware of this decision making. It happens unconsciously.

Takeaways

☑ When you want people to believe information, repeat it often.

☑ Using a related photo next to text increases the believability of information.

☑ When you use photos to augment information, assign someone on your team to be the fact-checker. Make sure the photos are accurate.

15 PEOPLE CHOOSE WHAT'S BRIGHTEST

Let's say you're the designer for an online grocery store. You're designing the product pages for a website or phone app. The people who will be using these product pages shop at the online store regularly. They're familiar with the products, and they have preferences for particular products and particular brands.

How much do their preferences influence their choice? Are they more of an influence than the visual design of the page? Is there anything you could do to make them choose one product over another? If you show pictures of the packaging (for example, a picture of the box of crackers), could the manufacturer do anything to increase the likelihood that someone would pick their product over another brand? Which is strongest: the individual's previous brand preference or something about the page or package design? Can you override an established preference based on visual design?

EXOGENOUS VS. ENDOGENOUS INFLUENCERS

Influences that are outside of people are called "exogenous (external) influencers"; influences from their preferences are called "endogenous (internal) influencers."

The "How People See" chapter described research showing that people use visual complexity and color when they are evaluating visual appeal, and that they make those judgments in less than one-half of a second (500 ms). But what happens when they're choosing from several products?

Milica Milosavljevic (2011 and 2012) searched for the answers to these questions in a series of studies. She had people rate their preferences for different snack food products, and then showed the products to them quickly on a screen. The participants had to decide which product they wanted to purchase.

Here's what Milosavljevic discovered:

- The visual brightness of the product packaging (called visual saliency in the research) was more important in the choice than the participants' preferences.

- If Milosavljevic slowed down the responses, either by asking participants to be confident before choosing, or having them choose with their hands rather than their eye gaze, then the visual saliency effect—choosing based on the brightness of the product package—was even greater.

So the endogenous factor of product preference can actually be overridden by an exogenous factor of making one product appear brighter than others on the screen.

The manufacturer could create a brighter package that would then translate into the image at the website. Or the designer could influence choice by making the product image brighter, or using additional visual attributes (boxes, borders, highlighting) to increase the visual saliency of a particular product.

Note The minimal time to make a product decision is around 313 ms. That's one-third of a second—even faster than the time to decide if a website is visually appealing.

Takeaways

☑ When you're designing a website or app and you want people to choose among different products or alternatives, make the product you want them to choose more "visually salient" than the others.

☑ Use the visual salience/brightness technique when you want to overcome the target audience's previous preference.

☑ Use the visual salience/brightness technique when you want your target audience to choose a product that is unfamiliar to them.

16 WHEN FACED WITH A COMPLEX DECISION, PEOPLE FOLLOW THEIR FEELINGS

You've probably had the experience of having to make a complex decision and getting advice like, "Don't let your feelings get in the way of making a good decision." Many people think the best way to make a complex decision is to rule out feelings.

As a designer, this idea that feelings get in the way of good decision making, and that people should base their decisions on solid, factual evidence, is likely to influence how, when, and how much information you build into your designs.

Let's say you work for a car company and your team is designing part of the website where potential customers can decide which vehicle they're interested in purchasing.

Or maybe you work for a company that sells software apps for email marketing, and you're designing the web page where people decide if they need the free package, the pro package, or the enterprise package.

Or maybe you work for an online university and you're designing an app that lets students sign up for courses for next semester.

All of these examples require people to make fairly complex decisions. Conventional wisdom holds that they'll probably base them on deliberation, rather than feelings.

If you follow that logic, then you, as the designer, would give your audience plenty of information about each choice, and make sure they have lots of time so they can make the best, and most deliberate, decision.

But that might be the opposite of what you should do if you want to help them make the best decision.

LOGIC OR FEELINGS?

Joseph Mikels (2011) conducted a series of studies to find out whether people make better complex decisions if they a) use logic, have comprehensive information, and carefully deliberate, or b) base the decisions on their feelings, with less information and less deliberation.

In his first study, he presented participants with attributes (things like gas mileage, safety features, and so on) for four hypothetical car options. Their task was to decide which was the best car. Before showing the car attributes and car options, Mikels told some of the participants to pay attention to, and base their decision on, which car was best, by focusing on the attributes they were about to see. He told other participants to pay attention to and base their decision on their feelings.

He reinforced the feelings versus information split by asking the participants in both groups different questions in the middle of the task. After showing an attribute about a car, the people with the feelings instructions were asked to rate how they felt about the particular car (they rated their feelings on a scale from 1 to 7, with 1 being very negative and 7 being very positive). The people in the information group were not asked about their feelings. Instead, they were asked how well they remembered the particular car (they too used a scale from 1 to 7, with 1 being "I don't remember anything about the car" and 7 being "I remember the car very well").

Half of the people went through this experiment for four cars and four attributes (simple condition) and half went through for four cars and 12 attributes (complex condition).

After they had viewed all the attributes and cars, Mikels asked each participant to choose which car was best, based on the attributes.

Lastly, he had each participant rate the importance of each attribute on a 7-point scale, with 1 being that the attribute—gas mileage, for example—was not important and 7 being that it was very important.

What were the results?

For this experiment, there *was* an actual best car: of the four cars, one had 75 percent positive attributes, two had 50 percent positive attributes, and one had 25 percent positive attributes—which means there was a "right" answer (that is, the car with 75 percent positive attributes).

For the simple condition (four cars, four attributes), there was no significant difference between the people who were given instructions to focus on feelings and the people who were told to focus on information. Both the feelings people and the information people performed similarly when picking the best car.

But there were significant differences for the complex condition (four cars, 12 attributes). Sixty-eight percent of the people in the feelings group picked the best car option, while only 26 percent of the information group chose the best car option.

Figure 16.1 shows the data.

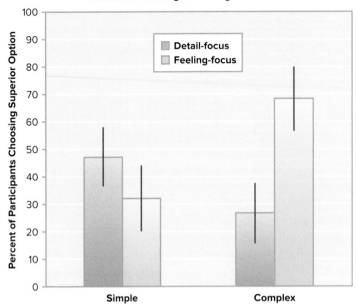

FIGURE 16.1 Feelings group versus information group results for simple and complex conditions.

SATISFACTION AND CONFIDENCE

Mikels ran the experiment again, but this time he had participants make only the complex decisions, and there was no objective "right" answer. Each of the four cars had half positive and half negative attributes. Instead of an objective right answer, he used importance ratings from each participant to determine the best choice for them.

In addition, he asked participants to rate how satisfied they were with their car choice (on a scale from 1 to 7, where 1 was not at all satisfied and 7 was extremely satisfied). He also asked how confident they were that they had made the best choice (on a scale from 1 to 7, where 1 was not confident and 7 was highly confident).

Again, the people in the feelings group made better car option decisions (based on their own importance ratings of attributes) than the people in the information group. Look at Figure 16.2. The feelings group not only made better decisions, but also were more satisfied with their choice and more confident that they'd made the right choice.

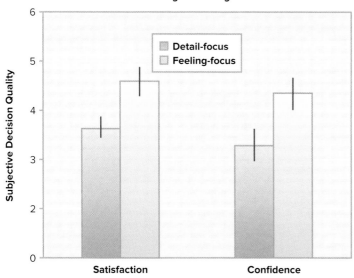

FIGURE 16.2 Satisfaction and confidence for the feelings and information groups.

WHAT ABOUT GIVING TIME FOR DELIBERATION?

We're not quite done with Mikels. In his third experiment in this series, he wanted to see if giving people time to deliberate made a difference. So he redid the experiment with the complex task only, but this time he assigned half of the participants to a "conscious deliberation" group and half to a "distraction" group. He told the conscious deliberation participants to think about the decision for 3 minutes before choosing a car. He gave the distraction participants a non-related working memory task for 3 minutes. (Look at random numbers that are shown for 2 seconds and respond if the number is the same number that appeared two trials before.) At the end of 3 minutes, both groups were told to choose one of the four cars as the best for them.

So what happened? Figure 16.3 shows the results.

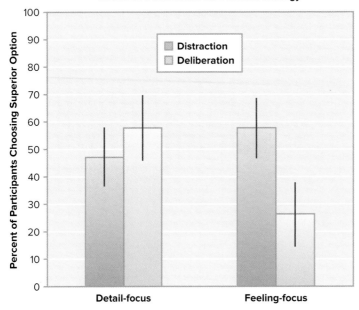

FIGURE 16.3 The results of distraction and deliberation.

- The people in the information group who were given 3 minutes to deliberate did as well as the people in the feelings group who did *not* deliberate. Taking time to think about a decision helped people when they were making a complex decision and had evaluated the information.

- The people in the information group who were distracted by an unrelated task did worse than those who just quietly deliberated.

- Doing an unrelated task didn't make a difference to the feelings group. They did as well as the information group. But when the feelings group was asked to deliberate on the decision, their accuracy plummeted.

DECISIONS FOR DESIGNERS ABOUT INFORMATION VS. FEELINGS

At this point you might be saying, "Wait, I can't do anything about this. I can't get inside someone's head when they're making a decision." True, but if you make design decisions about what and/or when information is provided, then your design can either help or hinder people's ability to make better decisions.

Here's what I draw from Mikels's research: If people have to make a complex decision, then you have two choices as a designer:

1. Give them just the critical information up front, tell them to focus on the information, and don't ask them to decide right away. Tell them to take a few minutes before they decide.

   or

2. Give them just the critical information up front, tell them to focus on how they feel rather than analyze the data, and then ask them to decide right away.

If you think that people will be using feelings to decide, then you definitely want to minimize the amount of time between when they have all the feeling information and when they decide.

THE BIG MISTAKE THAT MOST PEOPLE MAKE

Jim goes to a car website. He's trying to decide whether he should buy a new car now and, if so, whether it should be the XYZ brand, which model is the right one for him and his family, and whether he can afford it—a set of complex decisions.

When he gets to the website there's a picture of the car and it looks great (feeling). He watches the video of the family going on an adventurous vacation in the new car (feeling). He looks at the ratings for fuel efficiency and safety (information). He compares the different models through photos and data (information). Now he's ready to make a decision based on just the minimum amount of information he needed, and lots of feelings about which model is right for him and whether this car is right for him at this time.

So this is the golden moment. He's made the decision to buy and has chosen the model. This complex decision has been based mainly on feelings, and he hasn't had time to deliberate (which you now know through Mikels's work will only result in him making a bad decision). If you're the designer of this experience, then so far you've done a great job getting the person to make the best decision.

What you need to do next is get him to *commit* to the decision immediately. You should present a short form and get him to mark his decision. You could show a series of statements and have him choose the one that fits his decision:

"Yes, I've decided. The X model is the best car for me."

"I like the X model, but this isn't the right time for me to buy a car. I might buy at some point in the future."

"Thanks, but this is not the right car for me."

Get him to make a choice and then get him out of there. When he makes the choice, take him to a page that gives him the next step and tells him an email is on its way with a list of the closest dealers. The idea is to get him off the information-laden page before he starts looking at more information and deliberating.

If you're like most designers, you don't do this. Instead, you miss the golden moment. You don't ask him to decide and you don't get him off the page. Instead, you think, "We gave him all that engagement/emotion information and a few of the specs, now let's give him all the data so he'll see that this is the right decision." You start giving him detailed specs to review (wheel base, turning radius, 5-year maintenance and repair costs, ownership cost ratings). You cause a "deliberation" phase, and by doing so you significantly decrease the chances that he'll make a best decision.

Note Here's an important caveat. Mikels (2013) repeated his experiments a few years after the first series. He ran similar experiments with people whose average age was over 70. He found that older people are much more likely to use their intuition and feelings for decisions; in fact, they disregard the rational information too much. As a result, their feelings decisions about complex issues were often not the best choice.

Takeaways

☑ When you're presenting information to people under age 70 who have to make a complex decision, encourage them to use their feelings. In the middle of the process, ask them how they feel about the options.

☑ Even when you instruct people to use their feelings, you can't guarantee that they're using their feelings, so it's best to design the flow of information this way: a) Provide the minimum amount of information necessary, b) ask for the decision, and c) once they decide, stop providing them with information.

☑ When you're presenting information to people over age 70 who have to make a complex decision, don't encourage them to use their feelings.

☑ When you're presenting information to people who have to make a simple decision, give them the minimum amount of information necessary to make the decision and don't worry about instructions to use feelings, or preventing deliberation.

17 THE PUPILS DILATE DURING A DIFFICULT DECISION

There are several situations that will cause your pupils to dilate. For example, your pupils will dilate when you are attracted to someone or when you are in a low-light condition. Now researchers have found that pupil dilation is linked to the process of making difficult decisions. When this link was first noticed, researchers assumed that the pupils were dilating *after* a decision was made.

But Jan Willem de Gee (2014) has investigated whether the pupils actually dilate *during* the decision making process. The research team discovered that pupils dilate during decision making if the decision is a difficult one, and if the person is about to decide in a way that goes against previous beliefs.

This is interesting for designers to know. If you can determine whether a person is considering a decision that goes against what he usually does or believes, you can adjust what you're saying or showing to him.

For example, let's say you know someone usually buys Service Plan A, but you want to convince him to try Service Plan B. If you see that his pupils are *not* dilating, then you know you haven't convinced him to consider changing to the new plan. You could then show a particular video, image, or different information. If his pupils *are* dilating, then you know to stop presenting any more or new information and let him finish that deliberation and that decision.

Or, let's say it's time for your customer to renew his current service plan. If his pupils are dilating, then you know he's thinking about not renewing, or perhaps upgrading or downgrading the service plan. This would be a good time to show information about the advantages of staying the course and renewing.

You can also use pupil dilation to measure the effectiveness of your designs or campaigns. You could show people your design, product, or prototype, ask them to do tasks and make decisions, and see whether or not their pupils are dilating. You could then see when in the flow people are thinking about a decision that goes against what they usually believe, and you could test the idea of showing different information during the decision process to see if you can sway the decision.

Pupil dilation measurements are not too far in the future

If measuring pupil dilation sounds far-fetched, consider that pupilometers (small devices that measure pupil dilation) have been around for years. Most pupilometers don't have cameras to record dilation, but some do. Most eye-tracking equipment is capable of taking videos of the eye and some eye trackers already measure pupil dilation. The data on pupil dilation from eye-tracking machines isn't exactly easy to get or interpret, but this will likely improve. If you're not measuring pupil dilation in your user research now, you probably will be or could be soon.

Takeaways

☑ Consider using pupil dilation measures as a way to determine when your target audience is making a difficult decision, especially one that goes against what they usually think.

☑ If you're adventurous, think about how you could measure pupil dilation from built-in cameras on devices and how you could use that data to decide what to show next.

18 CONFIDENCE TRIGGERS DECISIONS

Why do people seem to make some decisions slowly and others very quickly? You might speculate that it's because sometimes they're deciding something small and insignificant, like what to order at a restaurant, and sometimes they're deciding something large and important, like whether or not to move to a new apartment or a new city. It seems natural to assume that important decisions would take more time.

But in reality, it's not the size of the decision that matters. The importance of the decision isn't what causes people to make up their minds quickly or slowly.

How about individual personality? Some people are spontaneous and others take a long time to decide everything. Although there are differences in personality (and brain chemistry) that cause some people to be more impulsive than others, even impulsive people sometimes take a long time to make decisions, and cautious people occasionally decide on things quickly. So it's not individual personality that predicts the time required to make a decision.

The best predictor of when someone is going to make a decision is how confident he is that he's made the best decision. And what's interesting is what affects that confidence.

THE EFFECTS OF EVIDENCE AND ELAPSED TIME

People make decisions when they're confident that they're making the "right decision." If they're not confident about their incoming information, then they won't make that "go" decision.

If people make decisions when they reach a certain level of certainty, the next question is what brings them to that moment of certainty? If your design is supposed to encourage people to make a decision (click on the Register button, download a file, press the Buy button), is there anything you can do to help people feel more certain and therefore speed up the decision-making process?

Research by Roozbeh Kiani (2014) investigated the relationship between certainty, elapsed time, and the amount of evidence.

When people are considering a decision, their brain networks (largely unconsciously) are not only analyzing all the factors and assessing the pros and cons of the decision, but also assessing how certain they are of making a decision at that point and how certain they are that the decision they're making is the best one. How do these decision-making brain networks decide if a person is certain? They use the person's past accuracy on decisions like this, and add to that information all the evidence, both pro and con, that the person has been accumulating for this particular decision.

Kiani specifically studied the effect that elapsed time has on the feeling of certainty. As time drags on and a person hasn't made a decision, the parts of the brain that are involved in decision making start to wonder if the person is taking a long time because the decision is difficult. The more time it takes, the more the network decides this must be a difficult decision. And if the decision is difficult, then the decision network becomes less certain that the person will make a good decision and that the person is ready to decide. Which of course puts the person into a loop (the longer it takes, the more difficult it must be and the less certain the person is, and therefore it takes more time).

CAN THE DECISION BE SPED UP?

Is it possible to change the perception of certainty or the elapsed time to get people out of this loop and encourage a decision? The answer is yes, and here's how to do it.

Since the decision network is looking at two things, elapsed time and amount of evidence, to decide about certainty, you can speed things up if you encourage the impression that a lot of evidence has accumulated.

Let's go back to the car website mentioned earlier. Jim is coming to the car site and looking at some information about particular car models. What could you do to make him feel that he has accumulated a lot of evidence? You could show him a lot of information—you could force him to view a series of pages about the cars. Then he could see that he has accumulated a lot of evidence. But that might take a lot of time, and if too much time elapses, then the decision network will lose certainty.

LITTLE CHUNKS AND LOTS OF FEEDBACK

Instead of providing a lot of information, the better tactic is to break the information into small chunks. Show the gas mileage as one independent chunk. Show the safety rating as one independent chunk. A lot of small chunks of information will give the decision network the impression that it has accumulated substantial evidence. Next, you can show the actual accumulation of those facts. Give feedback on the screen of all the information that has been accessed. You could display a running list of all the major topics Jim has looked at, or all the categories of information he has investigated.

Jim would now be looking at a screen that shows that he has already looked at car mileage, safety features, options, and the loan calculator. You don't have to show the data itself, just a checklist of the types of information he has accumulated.

The decision network will see the summary of all the information and perceive that a lot of evidence has been accumulated in a short amount of time. Remember, the amount of time that has elapsed is critical. If all that evidence has accumulated quickly, then the network in the brain will think that: a) the decision must not be that difficult, and b) plenty of evidence is there for certainty. This in turn will cause a feeling of certainty, and it's that feeling of certainty that will trigger the actual decision to act.

GET PEOPLE TO TAKE A PHYSICAL ACTION

It's not just one part of the brain that decides. There are portions of the brain that process information (for example, visual information or auditory information) and any of these areas can trigger the "I'm certain" idea, which in turn will trigger the decision to act. That decision to act will depend on what the action is, that is, reaching for something or clicking the mouse.

The motor (movement) parts of the brain are more involved in decision making than many people realize. You can increase the chance of a "go" trigger if you get people to take a physical action. They may not be ready yet for the actual "go" trigger, but if you can get them to take a series of smaller actions (click here to see the safety ratings, click here to choose the vehicle color), you increase the chance that they will more quickly take the final, larger "go" action.

Takeaways

☑ You can encourage the decision trigger-firing by organizing information into small chunks.

☑ Provide visual feedback of evidence as it accumulates—list all the pages, screens, or datapoints that have been considered during a session. This creates a feeling that evidence has accumulated quickly.

☑ Design the flow of tasks and screens so that your audience takes a series of small physical actions. The faster you get people to physically respond, the faster they reach the "go" trigger moment for the final decision.

19 THE SURPRISING EFFECTS OF STRESS ON DECISION MAKING

Josephine is the director of marketing at a genetics company. She loves her job, but it's very stressful. She's in charge of a new product launch, and the deadline is approaching. One of her best team members had to take a leave of absence for a medical emergency and she doesn't know when he'll be back. Things aren't likely to get less stressful for several months.

Josephine's husband, Alex, has a dilemma. His parents have been in poor health, and they've taken a turn for the worse. They live 500 miles away. Alex doesn't think his parents can live on their own in their house anymore, and there isn't a nursing home near where they live now. On the other hand, he doesn't think they'll want to move to the city where he and Josephine live, and neither he nor his parents can afford to pay for a nursing home in the city. He's the only child, so there's really no one else who can help out with his parents, or with these decisions about what to do.

Alex is an IT manager at a midsize financial investment firm. Sometimes his job is stressful, but right now the situation with his parents is even more stressful than his work.

What's likely to happen, then, if Alex brings up the idea about either moving to the small, rural village where his parents live, or finding another place to move where they can all live together in a larger apartment or house? Any of these changes will likely affect both his and Josephine's careers, as well as their living situation.

Alex feels that he can't wait much longer to have this conversation with Josephine, but she is under so much stress at work right now, he can't imagine asking her to make these decisions. He doesn't think she'll be able to come up with any good ideas given her current frame of mind and stress level, and he's reluctant to add to her troubles.

What should Alex do? Should he wait until Josephine's work stress goes down to have this conversation and make any big decisions? What effects will stress have on both Alex and Josephine's decision making?

THE COMPLICATED RELATIONSHIP BETWEEN STRESS AND DECISION MAKING

Mara Mather and Nichole Lighthall (2012) reviewed the research on stress and decision making. For their purposes, they defined stress as:

"Experiences that are emotionally or physiologically challenging" that "elicit sympathetic nervous system responses and stimulate the release of stress hormones (e.g., cortisol in humans) that mobilize the body's resources to respond to a challenge."

Physical stress and psychological stress affect both the dopamine reward pathways in the brain and the feedback loops that affect the assessment of risk and reward.

When making a decision under stress, people remember and apply what they've learned and experienced in the past that ended with a positive outcome. And they tend to ignore what they've learned or experienced in the past that ended with a negative outcome.

This means that if either Josephine or Alex have faced similar family-related and work-related stresses before and there was a positive outcome (they made some life or career changes, but it ended up being a good thing), they will remember those experiences now, while under stress, and those past, positive-ending experiences will influence the decisions they make now.

If they had similar experiences in the past that had a negative outcome (the life or career changes they made didn't advance them, but were negative), they will tend to forget about those experiences and those experiences will not influence the decisions they make now.

THE INTERESTING GENDER TWIST

But there's another consideration to take into account. It turns out that men and women react differently when a decision involves immediate risk-taking.

If people have to make an *immediate* decision while under stress, one that involves choosing between a safe option (less potential gain, but less risk of loss) or a riskier option (higher potential gain, but also higher potential loss), men tend to go for the riskier option and women tend to go for the safer option.

Figure 19.1 shows a flowchart of all these decisions.

So what does this mean for Josephine and Alex? If Alex brings it up now, and suggests that they move and look for new jobs right away, Josephine (being under a lot of stress) is likely to perceive this as an immediate risk and therefore go for whatever is the safer option for her. As mentioned earlier, they will both tend to remember similar decisions where things worked out well, but if Alex pushes for an immediate decision, Josephine will tend to go to safer options and Alex to riskier options.

Taking all of this into account, it would be best if Alex did one of two things:

1. Wait till Josephine is under less stress.

    or

2. Talk about it now, but not with the idea of having to make an immediate decision.

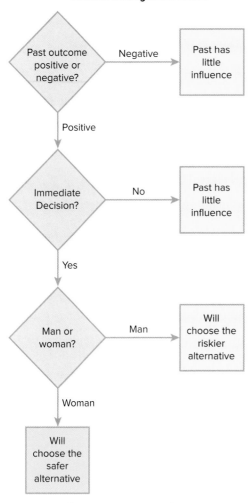

Decision-Making Under Stress

FIGURE 19.1   Decision making under stress.

IMPLICATIONS OF STRESS FOR DESIGN

So that was the summary of what Alex should do about talking to Josephine, but what are the implications of these stress effects for design?

Let's take an example:

You have a career website and app that help people take short- and long-term steps to a better career. You provide a comprehensive set of services, including advice, job searching, and help with preparing resumes and work portfolios.

People can use just a few of your services, or they can purchase a package of many services.

Some people who sign up for your services are men, and some are women. Some are under stress (just lost my job!) and others are not (wondering if this might be a good time to look around for a new position). If you knew their gender and their overall stress level, you'd be better able to advise them.

If people are under stress when they purchase your services, that's not necessarily a bad thing. If they've had any kind of similar positive experience, then the current stress might even help them make a decision to move forward.

In this situation, it would be useful for you to add in a customization part of your package. If you can get people to fill out a survey about stress level, and provide some data about their gender and past experiences with career moves, you could then create some algorithms that would help you help them.

For example, if you have a man using your app and he's currently under a fair amount of stress, but has had some positive experiences with career changes, then he'll be open to ideas for change. If, on the other hand, he hasn't had positive career change experiences, and he's under stress, then he'll be less likely to be open to big changes right now.

Takeaways

☑ When people are under stress as they make a decision, remind them of previous similar experiences they've had. When they recall similar experiences, they'll tend to remember only the positive experiences, and those positive experiences will make them more willing to make a decision.

☑ When your target audience is primarily women who are under stress, provide them with options that pose low risk. They're unlikely to choose an option that has high risk.

☑ When your target audience is primarily men who are under stress, provide them with options that have a high potential gain, even if those options include a high potential risk.

☑ When you're designing for a target audience of both men and women, provide options that are both safe and risky.

☑ When possible, try to determine the gender, past experience, and level of stress of your target audience, so you can customize your design accordingly.

20 PEOPLE MAKE DECISIONS AT CERTAIN CALENDAR EVENTS

You may want to pay attention to the month, day, and year that you advertise, promote, or recommend certain services or products. There are certain times in the calendar year, as well as certain years in life, when people are more disposed to making decisions and life changes. If you time your messages, events, and promotions, it's likely that they'll resonate more and that people will be more likely to make a change or purchase based on them.

Hengchen Dai, Katherine Milkman, and Jason Riis (2014) conducted a series of studies showing that people make commitments to personal improvement and change (dieting, gym memberships, eating healthier) on the first day or week of the new year, and on the first weekday after a federal holiday. (This research was conducted in the United States.) They call this the Fresh Start effect. Their theory is that these events give people a break from their usual routine and help them see a bigger picture of their lives, prompting a fresh start mindset.

In addition, Adam Alter and Hal Hershfield (2014) have a theory that big life decisions occur during milestone years, typically those ending in 9, such as 29, 39, 49, and 59.

Hershfield's theory is that it is at these times that people ask themselves reflecting questions, like "What am I doing with my life?" and that causes them to take action on big life decisions.

Alter and Hershfield analyzed data from an extramarital affairs dating site (ashley-madison.com), the US Centers for Disease Control and Prevention data on suicide, and a racing site (athlinks.com).

Of the 8 million men at the affair website looking for a date, more than 950,000 of the men were 29, 39, 49, or 59. That is 18 percent more than expected by chance. (Women showed the same trend, but it wasn't as strong as men.)

Of 500 marathon runners at the athlinks.com site (aged 25 to 64), 74 percent were in a year ending in 9.

And the suicide data from the CDC from 2000 to 2011 show that the suicide rate for both men and women between the ages of 25 and 64, who were in a 9 year was statistically significantly higher than other years.

Takeaways

When you design products or promotions related to exercise, health, wellness, or personal change:

☑ Schedule the launch to coincide with the first week of the New Year.

☑ Schedule the launch to coincide with the first weekday after a national holiday.

☑ Capture customer birthdates and then time your products and promotions to the people whose ages end with a 9.

21 PEOPLE MAKE DECISIONS BASED ON SPECIFIC MEMORIES

Let's return to Jim, who was looking into buying a new car. He's debating whether to get a small budget sedan or a larger sport utility vehicle with lots of bells and whistles. Psychologists have had two competing theories—the prototype theory and the exemplar theory—about how people think about decisions like these.

The prototype theory states that people have memories of different experiences, and that they create a general overview of those memories for a specific category. For example, if Jim thinks about deciding to buy the small sedan, he'll make that decision based on a general category overview of "small sedan."

The exemplar theory starts with the same idea—people have memories of different experiences—but it states that decisions are based not on a conglomerate overview category of memories, but on one or two specific memories. For example, if Jim thinks about deciding to buy the small sedan, he'll make that decision based on his memory of the road trip he took with his friend Linda in her small sedan and his mom's small sedan from when he was in high school.

The competing prototype and exemplar theories have been around for over 30 years. It was very difficult to devise an experiment to figure out which model was true until fMRI brain scanning became available. Michael Mack (2013) used fMRI brain scanning to test the two theories.

If the prototype theory is true, then the fMRI imaging should show activity patterns in some parts of the brain. If the exemplar theory is true, then the activity should show in different areas.

AND THE ANSWER IS...

A majority of the participants in the study showed brain patterns during decision tasks that matched the pattern you would expect if people were making decisions based on the exemplar model.

(For any of you who get into the details of brain science, Mack found that the posterior parietal cortex was the critical brain area for these memory/decision tasks. His theory is that the parietal cortex plays a critical role in encoding and retrieving exemplar memories for decisions.)

What does this mean for design? When people are making a decision, they're using specific memories to think about their decision. They're basing their decision not on generalities, but on specifics. If you know about their specific memories, you'll be better able to predict and even influence their decision.

For example, if you know that the only sedan your potential customer owned in the past was a gray Honda Accord, then you can assume that when he thinks about a sedan he's thinking about that gray Honda Accord. If he liked the gray Honda Accord, then you can talk to him about the new Honda Accords, or show him cars that are like them. You could show him photos of the new gray Honda Accord.

If you know that he didn't like the gray Honda Accord, and that he went on a fishing trip he really enjoyed with his friend in his friend's blue sport utility vehicle, then you can show him photos of a blue sport utility vehicle. His decision will be influenced by these specific memories.

You might be thinking: "Wait, I'm designing a website. I don't know what every visitor's memories of cars are. How can I possibly build that into the website"?

I admit that this takes a different way of thinking about design, and it requires some interesting changes. But imagine for a moment you've designed an interactive experience where a person comes to your car-buying website and is prompted to create a "past car parade." You ask him to talk about his first car. (Or if you don't want to go as futuristic as talking about his first car, then you can ask him questions that he answers just by choosing fields on the screen). Based on his answers, you bring up a picture of that car. You can also find out if he liked the car, and if he has good or bad memories of it. Then you go to the next car he owned or drove or spent time in. You keep going until there is a picture on his screen of all the cars he has had "relationships" with and liked.

If your customer is young and hasn't previously owned a car, then the car parade could include cars in which he had adventures, perhaps a parent's car or a friend's car.

Next, you could take him through a series of choices about the next car adventure he wants. You can start with photos from the car parade and, based on these photos and questions, you can predict, show, and help him refine the car he wants.

By doing this you're triggering specific memories and using those memories to guide him to a decision.

Takeaways

☑ In your design flow, ask people about specific memories and experiences with products or services in the past that match the products or services they're deciding on.

☑ Provide a summary of these experiences to trigger specific memories while they're making a decision.

22 BRAIN ACTIVITY PREDICTS DECISIONS BEFORE THEY'RE CONSCIOUSLY MADE

Imagine you're scanning music on your smartphone to decide what to listen to next. You're looking at a list of songs. You decide which song you want, and then you move your finger to touch the name of the song to start it playing. What's so interesting about that?

What's interesting is that your description of what happened isn't what actually happened.

Your experience is that:

1. You make a conscious decision about what song you want to hear.

2. You move your muscles to select the song.

But here's what really happens:

1. Unconscious parts of your brain make the decision of what song to listen to.

2. Those unconscious parts of your brain communicate the decision to other areas of the brain that control your motor movements.

3. Your arm/hand/finger start to move to execute the decision.

4. Information on what the decision was (finally) appears in your conscious brain areas.

5. You have the conscious experience of picking a song.

6. You use your finger to press the name of the song.

Brain scan research by Chun Siong Soon (2008) shows that it takes about 7 seconds from the time you make an unconscious decision to when your conscious brain thinks you have made the decision.

NOT JUST FOR MOTOR MOVEMENT

But what about decisions that don't involve motor movement? Maybe that 7-second lag is just for moving muscles.

Soon (2013) devised a different experiment to see if the same delay holds for making abstract decisions that don't involve simple motor movements. He found similar results. Up to 4 seconds before the person was aware of making a conscious decision, unconscious areas of the brain had made the decision and started acting on it. In this experiment, participants had to decide whether to work on a word task or an arithmetic task. Two areas of the brain would become active signaling that the decision had been made, but the participant would not yet be aware of the decision. In fact, parts of the brain having to do with working with words versus doing arithmetic tasks were alerted as soon as the decision was made, and still the participant wasn't aware that he or she had even decided.

The brain activity was so clear that researchers could not only see that a decision had been made, but also tell the participant what the decision was. The researchers knew what each person had decided before the person knew. Not only that, the researchers knew exactly *when* the decision would be made, as well as when the participant would consciously know that that the decision was made.

People who write about this research like to discuss the implications of this research: Is there really such a thing as free will? Is it possible to stop action on a decision after it's made, but before it's acted on and before the person even realizes he's decided? Is it possible to manipulate people's brains so they think the decisions they are making are their own, but in reality those decisions would be stimulated from the outside?

Although these are all interesting questions, they may not seem to be very practical from a design perspective.

But there *is* a practical impact of this research for designers: How much do we rely on what people say they did or say they are going to do? It's common for designers to interview their target audience for a product or service to find out things such as:

- How do you do this task currently?

- How do you go about making decisions about x?

- Do you prefer A or B?

- What would you do next?

- Which of these would you choose?

Designers ask target audiences these questions before designing, while designing, and after designing. Many have been taught that asking these questions of a target audience and acting on their answers is best practice for design and market research.

But Soon's research tells us that most—probably all—decisions and most mental processing of any kind happens unconsciously. So asking these questions and listening to answers that have been filtered through conscious thought may not be the best strategy. People don't actually know why they do what they do, or when they actually decided.

Your target audience will answer these questions as though they really know the answer, because they're unaware of all this unconscious processing going on. They can be very convincing with their answers of exactly what they thought and how they decided, and the exact moment they decided, because they really believe what they're saying, even though that's not actually how it happened.

Since few designers have access to expensive fMRI machines or the training to use them, we'll probably keep asking the questions. But it's important that we admit that answers don't actually tell us what is or will be going on in the brains of the target audience.

As tools for measuring brain activity become more sophisticated, they'll also become more affordable and easier to use. Eventually designers will all hook up test participants to machines to measure brain activity, heart rate, galvanic skin response, and so on. Some already are. There are some reliable biometrics tools available as I write this book, although some are still very expensive, and many are hard to learn to use.

Takeaways

☑ Refrain from making design decisions based entirely on what people *say* they would do. You can take this information into account, but don't use it as the basis for major design or redesign decisions.

☑ Watch how people actually interact with your products and services, then use this insight into their behavior to inform how to change them to better suit people's needs.

☑ Biometric equipment for body/brain measurements will only improve and become more affordable. Begin planning how and when you'll incorporate this feedback into your designs so you don't have to rely on the (faulty) conscious verbalizations of your target audience.

HOW PEOPLE READ AND INTERPRET INFORMATION

People learn to read at such a young age, and humans have been reading for centuries, so it's easy to forget that reading is a relatively new phenomenon. Because it's ubiquitous, it tends to be the go-to method for communicating online too. In this chapter, you'll find out that there are some interesting twists to how people read, and that reading may not be as straightforward as you think. Perhaps now is the time to embrace new ways to communicate information.

23 IF TEXT IS HARD TO READ, THE MATERIAL IS EASIER TO LEARN

For years, I—and most other designers I know—have believed, and written, and taught that if you want whatever you're designing to be easy to understand and use, then you have to make it easy to read. You have to use a font size that's large enough, a font type that's plain and not too decorative, and a background/foreground combination that makes it legible.

So imagine my surprise at discovering research—not just one study, but several—that shows that if text is *harder to read,* it's *easier to learn and remember.* Apparently being easy to read isn't the same thing as being easy to learn.

The underlying assumption that's been leading us astray is that reducing the cognitive load (the amount of thinking and mental processing) that people have to do is always a good thing. It is *often* a good thing, but instructional design theory has claimed for a long time that increasing the amount of work that people do to learn information often leads to deeper processing and better learning. Is it possible that hard-to-read fonts stimulate deeper processing?

THE INTERESTING TWIST OF DISFLUENCY

A term that learning psychologists use is "disfluency." Connor Diemand-Yauman (2010) defines this as:

> The subjective, metacognitive experience of difficulty associated with cognitive tasks

Disfluency is a feeling that something is difficult to learn. *Fluency* is a feeling that something is *easy* to learn.

Diemand-Yauman notes that when people feel that something is hard to learn, they process the information more deeply, more abstractly, and more carefully. The disfluency is a cue that they haven't mastered the material, and so they'd better pay more attention. The result is that they learn it better and remember it longer. Fluency, on the other hand, can make people overconfident, so they don't pay attention as well and they don't learn the material as deeply.

The chapter on How People Think and Remember talks about Daniel Kahneman's book *Thinking, Fast and Slow,* and about System 1 and System 2 thinking. When information is disfluent, people switch from automatic, intuitive easy thinking (System 1) into effortful and careful thinking (System 2). And this System 2 thinking helps them learn and remember.

Diemand-Yauman researched the idea that a hard-to-read font would lead to better learning and remembering. He gave participants information on three made-up species of space aliens. The participants had to read the material and learn about each species. Each alien species had seven features. (He was attempting to mimic what it's like to learn categories of animals in biology class, but trying to control for previous knowledge.)

Some of the participants were in the "disfluent condition." They read information about the alien species in 12-point, gray text. Some participants' text was in Comic Sans MS, and some was in Bodoni MT:

12-point, gray Comic Sans MS:

The smoshers

Three feet tall

Eats orange fruits

Has green eyes

12-point, gray Bodoni MT:

The smoshers

Three feet tall

Eats orange fruits

Has green eyes

Other participants were in a "fluent condition." They read the information in 16-point black Arial:

16-point, black Arial:

The temaphuts

Six feet tall

Eats green vegetables

Has blue eyes

Note   The examples above use the same fonts as the experiment, but the information itself is not exactly the same as the information used in the experiment.

Diemand-Yauman comments that although the font differences are obvious when the text is presented together in this way, since participants saw only one font, the effect was more subtle.

Participants had 90 seconds to memorize the seven pieces of information of all three alien types. Then they were asked to do other, non-related tasks as a distraction. And after that, they had a memory test for the alien information. For example, they were asked, "What does a temaphut eat?"

He found that people in the disfluent condition remembered significantly more information (14 percent more) than the people in the fluent condition. There was no difference between the two disfluent groups (Comic Sans and Bodoni).

Next Diemand-Yauman wanted to see if the same effect would be true in a more realistic setting. He took the study to a high school (in Ohio in the United States) and tested 220 students. He screened the classes for those where the same teacher had been teaching at least two classes of the same subject and difficulty level and with the same learning material. The experimenters took all the worksheets and PowerPoint slides and changed the font. (The experimenters did not meet the teachers or the students or visit the class.)

Classes were randomly assigned to either a disfluent or a control category. The disfluent classes used material that was switched to one of these fonts:

Haettenschweilor

Monotype Corsiva

Comic Sans Italic

In the control classes, no changes were made to the fonts. Teachers and students didn't know the hypothesis that was being studied. They didn't know whether they were in a fluent or disfluent group. The material was taught the same way it normally was taught. No other changes were made in the classrooms or the instruction.

Students in the disfluent condition scored significantly higher on their regular classroom tests. On a survey asking if they liked their course or course material, there were no differences in these preference ratings. There was no difference among the different disfluent fonts.

SO, WHAT'S A DESIGNER TO DO ABOUT FONTS?

If you design textbooks or e-learning modules, then this research has direct relevance to you. But what about people who design other things, like websites, instructions, or product packaging? What if you're putting out a series of marketing emails? What should you do about fonts?

You might be tempted to make a distinction between what people are reading for information and what they're reading in order to learn and remember. But that may not be as simple a distinction as it sounds. If people are reading a blog post about current events, are they "just reading"? Don't they want to understand, learn, and remember the information?

I can't make myself recommend that you use a font that's slightly harder to read than you're used to if you want people to learn and remember your content. However, that's what I *should* say.

 Learn better or believe more?

The research on disfluency has to be applied carefully. So far this chapter has talked about learning information and remembering it. If you're trying to convince people that something is *true*, then you're better off making it easy to read. In the chapter on How People Decide, you learned about "truthiness"—the idea that some things *feel* more true.

Back in 1999, Rolf Reber and Norbert Schwarz showed that text written in different colors on different backgrounds influenced whether people believed the information. Participants found information in hard-to-read background/foreground colors, like this,

Brazil nuts are a good source of the trace mineral selenium

to be less believable than information in easier-to-read colors.

Takeaways

☑ When the most important goal is for people to believe that what they're reading is true, make the text as legible as possible, using a simple font and plenty of contrast between the text and the background.

☑ When people already believe the information and the most important goal is for them to learn and remember it, consider using a font that's slightly harder to read. If the font is slightly harder to read, then people will learn and remember the information better.

24 NOUNS SPUR ACTION MORE THAN VERBS SPUR ACTION

If you've ever had to name a button on a website, app, or landing page, then you've probably had the moment where you're going back and forth between options. "Sign up" or "Register"? "Order" or "Shopping cart"?

Is there a way to word these requests, actions, or buttons that encourages people to take action?

Gregory Walton at Stanford studies connectedness and affiliation between people. In a series of experiments, he tested how different labels affect behavior.

Psychologists, and people in general, tend to think that preferences and attitudes are stable. People like opera or they don't. People like to go dancing or they don't.

Walton thought these attitudes and preferences might not be so stable after all. Maybe how people think of themselves—and how that influences their behavior—is more temporary and fluid. And maybe whether they act, or not, can be influenced by labels.

He conducted a series of experiments to test this out. In the first experiment, participants evaluated the preferences of others described with noun labels or with verbs:

"Jennifer is a classical music listener."
or
"Jennifer listens to classical music a lot."

He tested a wide variety:

Author
X is a Shakespeare reader.
X reads Shakespeare a lot.

Beverage
X is a coffee drinker.
X drinks coffee a lot.

Dessert
X is a chocolate eater.
X eats chocolate a lot.

Mac/PC
X is a PC person.
X uses PCs a lot.

Movie
X is an Austin Powers buff.
X watches Austin Powers a lot.

Music
X is a classical music listener.
X listens to classical music a lot.

Outdoors
X is an indoor person.
X spends a lot of time indoors.

Pet
X is a dog person.
X enjoys dogs a lot.

Pizza
X is a Pepe's pizza eater.
X eats Pepe's pizza a lot.

Sleeping time
X is a night person.
X stays up late.

Sports
X is a baseball fan.
X watches baseball a lot.

Walton tried to use statements that are used in conversation, for example, "Beth is a baseball fan," and "Beth watches a lot of baseball." He didn't use "Beth is a baseball watcher," even though that's technically a better word match.

He found that when people read nouns to describe other people's attitudes they judged those attitudes to be stronger and more stable than when the attitudes were described with the verbs.

In a second experiment, he used similar sentences and had people describe themselves. People would fill in the blanks, for example:

Dessert
I'm a _____ lover. (chocolate . . .)
I eat _____ a lot. (chocolate . . .)

Mac/PC
I'm a _____ person. (Mac/PC)
I use _____ a lot. (Mac/PC)

Outdoors
I'm an _____ person. (outdoors/indoors)
I spend a lot of time _____. (outdoors/indoors)

After the participants had filled in the blanks, Walton asked them to rate their strengths and preferences. For example, on a scale from 1 to 7:

"How strong is your preference for this topic?"

"How likely is it that your preference for this topic will remain the same in the next five years?"

"How likely is it that your preference for this topic would remain the same if you were surrounded by friends who did not enjoy what you prefer?"

The results were similar to the first experiment. When there were regular nouns, participants evaluated their preferences as being stronger. Unusual or made-up nouns "baseball watcher" did not have the same effect.

TO VOTE? OR TO BE A VOTER?

Christopher Bryan and Gregory Walton (2011) conducted additional studies to see if this idea of nouns and verbs would affect voting.

They contacted people who were eligible to vote, but hadn't registered yet (in California in the United States). The participants completed one of two versions of a brief survey.

One group of participants answered a short set of questions that referred to voting with a noun:

"How important is it to you to be a voter in the upcoming election?"

Another group answered similar questions worded with a verb:

"How important is it to you to vote in the upcoming election?"

The researchers' hypothesis was that using the noun would create more interest among the participants, and that they'd be more likely to register to vote.

After completing the survey, the participants were told that to vote they would need to register and they were asked to indicate how interested they were in registering.

Participants in the noun group expressed significantly more interest (62.5 percent) in registering to vote than participants in the verb group (38.9 percent).

Bryan and Walton didn't stop there. They recruited California residents who were registered to vote but hadn't yet voted by mail. They used the same noun and verb groups the day before or the morning of the election.

They then used official state records to determine whether or not each participant had voted in the election. As they had predicted, participants in the noun condition voted at a significantly higher rate than participants in the verb condition (11 percent higher).

They ran the test again in New Jersey for a different election and, again, the people in the noun group voted more than those in the verb group.

INVOKING A GROUP IDENTITY

I have a theory about this, too. In *How to Get People to Do Stuff,* I wrote that everyone has a need to belong. Using a noun invokes group identity. You're a voter, or you're a member, or you're a donor. When you ask people to do something and phrase it as a noun rather than a verb, you're invoking that sense of belonging to a group and people are much more likely to comply with your request.

Takeaways

☑ When naming a button on a form or landing page, use a noun, not a verb: "Be a member" or "Be a donor" instead of "Donate now."

☑ When writing a description of a product or service, use nouns instead of verbs. For example, say, "When you're ready to be an expert, check out our training courses," rather than "Check out our training courses."

☑ Use common nouns. Don't make up words just to have a noun.

25 HOMOPHONES CAN PRIME BEHAVIOR

You are, unfortunately, working late at night again. You have a report due in the morning but it isn't quite done, so you're sitting in your home office trying to finish it.

You decide to take a short break from the report and read one of the blogs you try and keep up with. You read a post from a well-known journalist who is about to leave on a trip overseas. He writes a kind of farewell post and at the end he signs it "Bye!" On the blog page, you see an ad for the journalist's latest book with a "Buy now" button. You click and buy his book.

Next, you're skimming a news site and you see a headline: "Is the Fed Chairman Right?" Suddenly you realize it's getting late and you haven't finished writing your report. You get back to work.

Was any of your behavior during that interlude "primed"?

Priming is when exposure to one stimulus influences your response to another stimulus. In the example above, you were primed with the word "Bye" (first stimulus) at the end of the blog post you read. Your exposure to "Bye" then affected your response to the second stimulus—"Buy" that was on the "Buy now" button.

That's not all. Your exposure to the word "Right" (another stimulus) in the news headline primed you to think of the word "write" (the last stimulus), and made you realize you were supposed to be writing your report.

PRIMING WITH HOMOPHONES

Psychologists and marketing researchers have known about the effects of priming for decades. But realizing that priming works with homophones is a new discovery.

A homophone is a word that has the same pronunciation as another word, but a different meaning, and sometimes a different spelling. Here are some examples:

Bye/buy

Write/right

Carrot/carat

Air/heir

Brake/break

Cell/sell

Cereal/serial

Coarse/course

Fair/fare

Know/no

One/won

Profit/prophet

Derick Davis and Paul Herr (2014) wanted to see if homophones would act as primes, and if so, how strongly and under what conditions. Their idea was that homophones would activate the meaning and association of the related homophone, and that this activation would affect behavior. If people saw the word "bye," they'd be more inclined to buy something.

PEOPLE SUBVOCALIZE WHEN READING

When people read, they subvocalize—that is, they speak words internally. These words activate memories associated with the words. When people read the word "bye," they associate meanings such as leaving or going on a trip. But because people subvocalize and say the word to themselves, Davis and Herr hypothesized that the association for the homophone "buy" would also be activated, and that the associations would stay in memory for a short time. (Since homophone priming is based on subvocalizing, this entire effect is different for every language.)

SUPPRESSING HOMOPHONE ACTIVATION

Research on reading has shown that a lot of the time people automatically and unconsciously suppress the activation of homophone associations. The better a reader a person is, the more she suppresses the associations.

So if you're a pretty good reader, you might be less susceptible to homophone priming—unless you're under a high cognitive load.

 It's a myth that good readers don't subvocalize

If you've ever taken a speed-reading course, you may have been told that subvocalizing will slow down your reading. Don't confuse moving your lips with subvocalizing. It may slow you down to move your lips while you read, but everyone subvocalizes (no sound, no movement). In the case of the homophone effect, it's not that better readers aren't subvocalizing. It's that better readers don't have as many automatic homophone associations.

THE COGNITIVE LOAD GOTCHA

It takes some cognitive work to suppress homophone activation. This means that as you become more mentally busy—as your cognitive load increases—your susceptibility to the homophone priming increases, too.

Let's go back to the example of working on the report late at night and encountering the homophones. Since you're working late and you have a deadline the next day, it's possible that you have a fairly high cognitive load, which would make you susceptible to the bye/buy homophone activation.

EMBEDDED HOMOPHONES HAVE THE SAME PRIMING EFFECT

In their research, Davis and Herr tested embedded homophones too, such as "good-bye" and "bye" or "good buy." They found the embedded homophones followed the same priming activation as single homophones.

HOMOPHONE ACTIVATION IS UNCONSCIOUS

Davis and Herr tested 860 participants in their homophone research. None of the participants were aware of the homophone activation that had occurred.

 Order sometimes matters for homophone activation

Homophones activate each other most when both words are common words (buy/bye). But if one of the words isn't that common (you/ewe), then the order matters for activation. If you see "you" first, you're unlikely to have "ewe" activated (unless you're a sheep farmer). However, if you see the word "ewe," it's likely that "you" would be activated.

AN ETHICAL DILEMMA?

So here's one of those times when designers have an ethical dilemma. Do you purposely try to get people to do something by messing with homophones? Do you put the word "bye" in your blog post or on your website not too far from the word "buy" in a different context? Do you not only sprinkle the priming homophone, but also up the cognitive load on the page so the person will be even more susceptible? Should I have even included this information in this book if it means that some people will now use it to get people to take an action that's not in their best interest?

I'm often asked about ethics in my work, because so much of the research I talk about has to do with how to get people to take action. It's something I think about a lot, although I don't have a quick answer. The basic question is: "If we use this information from behavioral science research to get people to do what we want them to do, are we being too manipulative? Are we being ethical?"

One point of view is that if you're trying to get people to do something, no matter what it is, then that *is* unethical. Another is that if you're trying to get people to do something that's good for them (eat healthier, quit smoking), then it's OK. I fall somewhere between these two ideas.

My take on the research I talk and write about is that these effects are powerful. However, there's a limit. Using these behavioral science influences won't give you total control over the other person. I also believe that each designer has to decide for himself or herself where the line is between influence and ethics. Every time you design something, you have to decide where that line is. Here's some idea on where my line is usually drawn:

I don't completely agree with the people who say that it's OK to use these techniques to change behavior related to eating, smoking, or conserving energy—things that help the individual or help society—but it's not OK to get people to buy a new refrigerator. Trying to change behavior is trying to change behavior.

I've been an expert witness/consultant for the US government on cases involving internet fraud, and this has given me some insight into where the line is on ethical and unethical behavior. Putting your product or service in its best light, and matching your product or service with the needs and wants of your customers—these are OK. Does everyone really need a new refrigerator? Probably not. But encouraging them to buy a new refrigerator now, and to buy it from you, is perfectly fine. Otherwise, we might as well proclaim that *all* marketing and advertising is unethical, which is probably an opinion some of you have!

Purposely deceiving people, giving them confusing instructions so they don't know what they've agreed to, encouraging them to engage in behavior that harms them or others, or trying to get them to break the law—these are not OK.

Interestingly, homophone priming falls right in the middle of those two places on the continuum. This means that in the work that I do I wouldn't use homophone priming to get people to take the action I want them to take.

As I said, you'll have to decide for yourself.

Takeaways

☑ You can use homophones to affect people's behavior.

☑ When you want to increase the power of the homophone effect, increase people's cognitive load.

☑ People are not aware of the homophone priming effect. Think carefully about the ethics of this technique. Don't use it if you find it to be unethical.

26 PEOPLE READ ONLY 60 PERCENT OF AN ONLINE ARTICLE

That is, if they read it at all.

CLICKING DOESN'T MEAN READING

As the CEO of Chartbeat, a company that analyzes real-time web analytics, Tony Haile (2014) has seen a lot of data on what people are doing online.

In the advertising world, clicks were king for a long time. A lot of money has changed hands over pay-per-click and page views, both of which measure the success of online advertising by counting clicks. Haile says that's the wrong measurement.

Haile looked at 2 billion online interactions, most of them from online articles and news sites, and found that 55 percent of the time people spend less than 15 seconds on a page. This means they're not reading the news articles.

Chartbeat's data scientist, Josh Schwartz, analyzed scroll depth on article pages. Most people who come to an article scroll through 60 percent of it. Ten percent never scroll, which means they're not reading much.

Haile says instead of clicks, we should concentrate on the amount of attention the audience gives, and whether they come back.

Some organizations, such as Upworthy, have started using a metric of "attention minutes."

SHARING DOESN'T EQUAL READING

Another action that's sought after is sharing on social media. The assumption is that if people share an article, for example, on Facebook, or tweet about it on Twitter or mention it in a LinkedIn post, they've read what they're sharing, right?

The relationship between reading and sharing is weak. Articles that are read all the way through aren't necessarily shared. Articles that are shared have likely not been read past 60 percent.

According to Adrianne Jeffries (2014), Buzzfeed and Upworthy, two popular article sites as I write this book, report that most tweets occur either at 25 percent through the article or at the end of the article, but not much in between those two extremes.

Takeaways

☑ Don't assume people are reading the whole article.

☑ Put your most important information before the 60 percent point of the article.

☑ When you want people to share the article, remind them to do that about 25 percent of the way through the article and again at the end.

☑ Don't assume that if people shared the article that means they read all or even most of it.

27 READING ONLINE MAY NOT BE READING

One of the ideas I talk about a lot when I give keynotes is that technology changes quickly but humans don't. Most of the ways that people's eyes, ears, bodies, and brains work has come about from eons of evolution. And these aren't likely to change quickly.

I did say *most*. Reading is an exception. And that's because reading is not hardwired. Every brain has to learn how to read.

Maryanne Wolf, the director of the Center for Reading and Language Research at Tufts University, wrote a book called *Proust and the Squid: The Story and Science of the Reading Brain*. In it she explains that people's brains weren't made to read. Unlike the capacity to walk or talk, reading is not built in. It's something people learn to do, and, interestingly, there isn't just one way that the brain reads.

NEUROPLASTICITY AND READING

People's brains change throughout their lives. The term that's used is neuroplasticity. The brain reorganizes itself. It forms new neural connections, and sometimes changes where in the brain certain functions occur. This is in response to the environment and what people do each day. Learning to read causes the brain to change, too.

In some ways, people's brains change in predictable ways when they learn to read, regardless of the language. Kimihiro Nakamura (2012) mapped brain activity with fMRI scans for people who learned to read in French versus Chinese. He found that there are two circuits, one for shape recognition by the eye and another for gesture recognition system by the hand, which are activated and show the same pattern of activity with both languages.

There are some differences in the pattern of activity, though, based on language. For example, there's more activity in the gestural areas of the brain for people who read Chinese, compared to French. No matter what the language people read in, however, their brains change when they learn to read. As Wolf points out, parts of the brain that are hardwired for other tasks—for example, shape recognition, speech, and gesturing—create new circuits and neuron connections when people learn to read.

SKIMMING AND SCANNING VS. READING

The type of reading people do when they sit down—focused and not distracted—to read a book (whether on an e-reader or on paper, whether a novel or nonfiction) is quite different from the type of reading they do when they're browsing information online. They use different parts of the brain.

People think differently when they're doing focused reading. Good readers do what Wolf calls "deep reading." They think while they read. They connect what they're reading to their own experiences. They come up with new ideas. They go beyond what the author is writing to interpret and analyze. They're having an *internal* experience.

Skimming and scanning are a different experience—not worse, just different. People use more visual attention when they skim and scan. They internalize much less. It's an *external* experience. These differences between deep reading and skimming and scanning show up on brain image scans.

DESIGNING FOR SKIMMING AND SCANNING IS BEST PRACTICE, RIGHT?

If you're designing products that involve people reading text, you're probably aware that many people don't read everything they see on a screen. And you're probably aware that you need to break text up into smaller chunks, and use headings. These guidelines have been accepted as best practice for online text for several years. However, I'm going to suggest that you think about this in a more radical way than you might be used to.

IT'S NOT READING

Based on this new research on deep reading, skimming, and scanning, I'm recommending that you stop thinking of what people do when they go to a website or read an online article as reading. (The exception is when people are reading a book with an online reading device.)

I'm suggesting that reading be defined as follows:

When people sit or stand in one position with little movement and read text on a digital or paper page, when they are not distracted by anything else on the page or anything in their environment, when the only interaction with the device or paper product is to go to the next page or, now and then, go to a previous page, and when they maintain this activity for at least 5 minutes without doing anything else—that is reading.

Anything else involving the processing of words on a screen or a page is skimming and scanning.

DESIGNING FOR SKIMMING AND SCANNING

Most people who design websites, apps, and products aren't designing for reading as I've described it above. My premise is that you're designing for an activity that's not reading. Skimming and scanning looks different in brain scans from reading. Skimming and scanning are external experiences, based on visual attention.

If you're designing for skimming and scanning, assume that people are not thinking deeply about what's written, they're probably reading very little of it, they're skipping over large parts, and they're not interpreting and analyzing the information.

READING IS CHANGING = BRAINS ARE CHANGING

One more thought: people skim and scan when that's appropriate and they deep read when that's appropriate. How wonderful it is that the human brain is plastic enough to learn both, and can change from one to the other when needed.

This switch from reading to skimming and scanning is no problem for people who grew up learning how to deep read, and then, later, learned how to skim and scan. Is it possible that new generations will grow up without learning deep reading at an early age? Or that they may learn skimming and scanning first, and then deep reading? Or maybe they won't ever learn deep reading?

Wolf hypothesizes that since this brain reorganizing alters the way people think, these changes could have large and unanticipated consequences for how people interact with information. Will humans get to the point where they don't analyze information they're "reading" because they're skimming and scanning, not reading? Will people get to the point where they don't have an internal experience when taking in words?

Takeaways

- ☑ People are probably skimming and scanning your online text, so make sure you follow skimming and scanning guidelines: break information into small bits and use headings.

- ☑ Don't assume that people have "read" online text.

- ☑ Don't assume that people have comprehended or remembered online text.

- ☑ Minimize the amount of text you use online.

28 THE MULTISENSORY EXPERIENCE OF PHYSICAL BOOKS IS IMPORTANT TO READING

Many people now do some of their reading (as defined in the previous section) on paper and some on an e-reader, and maybe some on a tablet. The world seems split these days between people who like reading physical books and those who prefer reading on a device.

Even with e-readers that use electronic ink and therefore have a different screen than a tablet, is reading an e-reader a different experience than reading a physical book? Does the sensory experience of reading a book make a difference? If so, in what way?

THE MULTISENSORY EXPERIENCE OF PHYSICAL BOOKS

A human factors scientist talks about the tactile experience when talking about touch. The design of tactile experiences is called "haptics," which refers specifically to applying tactile sensation to a human-computer interaction.

There are many differences in the tactile experience of reading a physical book and the current haptic of reading on an e-reader or tablet. Even though the ink on the page may be similar, books have other tactile features that the haptic interface on an e-reader doesn't have, at least as of the time I'm writing this book.

A physical book has weight, and the feeling of weight is different from book to book. The physical weight affects people's perception of the importance of the work. Research on embodied cognition shows that when people hold something heavy, they think it is more important. With an e-reader, all books weigh the same amount. The same is true of a thin book versus a thick book. The number of pages and the thickness of a physical book is part of the experience of the book.

When you read a book, you can feel the paper. Turning the pages of a book requires a different movement than turning the pages of an e-reader. The pages of a physical book make a sound when you turn the page. There's a sound when you close the cover of a large, hardcover book.

You can even smell some books. I was a reader at an early age, and the smell of old books can still take me back in my memory to being a young child in the public library with my mother, running my hands over the spines of old novels, excited about what I would read.

Reading a physical book is a multisensory experience that involves touch, smell, sight, and sound. E-readers involve touch and sight, but they're the same for all books;

there's some sound, but not like a physical book, and no smell. You'll have to do a lot of interesting design to make the experience of an e-reader as rich as the experience of a physical book.

Don't get me wrong. I'm not a Luddite. I love my e-reader. But I know that it's not the same as a physical book.

THE NAVIGATION AND MENTAL MAP OF A BOOK

People can navigate physical books in a way that they can't with an e-reader. A physical book is like a landscape. People map a physical book when they're reading. Their memory of a certain section is tied to the physicality of the book. If I ask you, "Where's the passage in the book where John expresses his doubts about Adam's competency as a doctor?," you'll probably turn to a spot about one-third in from the front. You might say, "I remember seeing that at the bottom of one of these pages on the left." Your memory of the book is a physical memory. That type of physical "mapped" memory of reading doesn't occur with e-readers.

Physical books have what Ferris Jabr (2013) calls a "topography" that e-readers don't. When you have a book open, you have left and right pages. There are eight corners you can reference. You can see where you are in relation to the edges of the book, the corners, how far you've read on a page, and how far you've read in the book. Jabr says that these cues make it easy to not only navigate, but also create a mental map of the text.

When you read a book on an e-reader, a smartphone, a tablet, or a monitor, you don't have these navigation cues and you don't have that mental map. You can navigate, but not in an intuitive way that creates a mental map.

LIMITED NAVIGATION IMPAIRS COMPREHENSION

Anne Mangen's (2013) research study in Norway had tenth graders of similar reading ability read and study a narrative passage (a story, either fiction or nonfiction) and an expository passage (text that explains, not in story form). Each passage was about 1,500 words long. Half the students read the passages on paper, and the other half read them as PDF files on a computer with a 15-inch LCD monitor. After reading the passages, the students took a reading comprehension test with both multiple-choice and short-answer questions. During the test, they could refer to the passages. Students who read the texts on the computers had lower scores on the test than students who read the texts on paper.

Mangen watched the students reference the passages during the test. Students who worked with PDFs had more difficulty finding information. Those who read on paper held the paper in their hands and could quickly switch between pages. They could easily find the beginning, middle, and end, or anywhere in between.

Some research shows that students who read textbooks on a computer don't remember the information as well in the long term. There's a difference between "remembering" and "knowing." When people "remember," they recall a particular piece of information, and they often also recall the situation around it—where they were, where they learned it from, and so on. When people "know" something, they feel that it's true, but they may not remember how they learned it. One theory by Kate Garland, a researcher at the University of Leicester, is that remembering is a weaker type of memory than knowing. Memories fade and knowing stays. Garland's idea is that when students read on paper, they learn the material more thoroughly, which helps it turn into "knowing."

SCREENS ARE HARDER ON THE EYES

When you read text on paper, the paper reflects the light in the room. This is called ambient light. If you're using an e-reader with e-ink, that also reflects ambient light. But if you're reading on a computer monitor, smartphone, or tablet, you're not using ambient light, at least as of the writing of this book. The light coming from a screen is harder to read and causes eyestrain.

Some researchers hypothesize that people learn or remember less information when reading from screens because they have to spend more visual energy reading the screen than they would reading a book.

WILL PEOPLE JUST GET USED TO IT?

Because reading is something the brain learns to do, it's possible that reading on devices is also something that our brains will get used to doing. It's too early to know whether some of the disadvantages that researchers currently see for reading online compared to physical books are because reading online is less effective, or if people who grow up reading online first, or only reading online, will have brains that adapt.

THE ROLE OF THE DESIGNER

Designers have created some innovations in online reading, such as e-ink, but in many ways we haven't really designed an online reading experience. We just took letters and pictures and put them on a screen. The hardware is new and sometimes innovative, but the experience isn't. Experience designers need to dig deeper into what reading is, and what books are, to build some of the multisensory aspects of reading a physical book into digital reading devices. We need to not just add features, like highlighting, but apply innovative design thinking to reimagine the whole idea of digital books and digital reading. (Where's my Harry Potter newspaper?)

In the meantime, we need to think about how best to deal with asking people to read online. If the experience is just OK, if it hampers learning and hurts people's eyes, maybe we shouldn't ask people to do it as much as we do. You'll learn about some alternatives in the next section.

Takeaways

- ☑ When designing a product that requires people to read online text, don't assume they'll remember what they read as well as when they read a physical book.

- ☑ Rethink your use of text. Is it necessary to have people do so much reading online?

- ☑ Since online books lose navigational cues, consider building in additional ways of navigating text online. Make sure it's easy for people to go back, go forward, mark a section, and search.

29 PEOPLE ARE READY TO MOVE ON FROM "OLD" MEDIA

Here's something that's at least a little ironic: if reading is so unnatural, maybe we should let it go.

I say ironic because I'm an author. I write books with words in them and assume (and hope) that people will read them. So it doesn't really make much sense for me to say that we should let reading go. I have a lot of videos that I use to teach behavioral science and design, but, as you can tell, I still rely quite a bit on the written word for communicating.

If we're not going to eliminate reading altogether, then maybe we should confine ourselves to physical books and just stop asking people to read on screens. If, as you've seen in this section of the book, reading is problematic as a way to communicate on-screen, then what are the alternatives?

VIDEO AND AUDIO ALTERNATIVES

Visual content with some kind of audio is one effective form of online communication that's currently available. I don't mean to sound vague, but there are many possible combinations, and they can all be effective.

For example, a video that has a talking head image (a video of the person) with the audio of the person talking is one combination. If the person who's being filmed has poor speaking or on-camera stills, it's less than perfect, but it's probably more effective than reading. Why is that? There are several reasons:

1. The fusiform facial area (FFA) of the brain analyzes and interprets faces. So people are predisposed to pay attention to faces. Faces grab people's attention. The FFA also interprets the emotional information from the face, so people get added emotional content when they watch a talking head video.

2. People get a lot of information from hearing someone talk. There is, of course, the content of what the speaker is saying, but there's additional information contained in what's called the paralinguistics of speech. Paralinguistics consist of prosody (patterns of intonation) and emotional content.

3. Gestures and facial expression tell the viewer how the speaker feels.

4. Movement in peripheral vision grabs attention. If people watch a video of someone talking, they notice the speaker's gestures—even if the gestures are subtle. (Refer to the chapter on How People See for more about peripheral vision.)

5. Speakers and listeners' brains sync up. When people listen to someone talking, the brain starts working in sync with the speaker. In his research study, Greg Stephens (2010) put participants in an fMRI machine and had them record or listen to recordings of other people talking. He found that when participants listened to someone else talk, the brain patterns of the two people started to couple, or mirror each other. There was a slight delay, which corresponded to the time it took for the communication to occur. Several different brain areas were synced. He compared this with having people listen to someone talk in a language they did not understand. In that case, the brains did not sync up.

    The more the brains were synced up, the more the listener understood the ideas and message from the speaker. The parts of the brain that have to do with social interaction were also synced. Social communication is critical to understanding the beliefs, desires, and goals of others.

    A video of someone talking is more powerful than just reading words on a page.

6. There's a special part of the brain for processing the human voice. Although people aren't born ready to read, they are born ready to interpret the human voice, including the emotional information conveyed by speech.

 Dogs and humans have similar voice-processing areas

Attila Andics (2014) took fMRI brain scans of dogs and people. He had them listen to both dog and human sounds, including crying, laughing, and barking. The dogs showed a similar voice-processing area of the brain as the humans, in a similar location. Dogs and humans showed similar brain activity when they listened to voices with positive emotions (laughing), and less activity when hearing negative emotions (crying or whining). Both dogs and humans responded more to their own species.

Victoria Ratcliffe and David Reby (2014) discovered that dogs break human speech into two parts—the emotional cues and the meaning of the words—and these different kinds of information are processed in different parts of the brain, similar to humans. For the most efficient interpretation, Ratcliffe recommends speaking emotional information to a dog's left ear and commands to its right ear.

Emotions are contagious

When people are excited, happy, sad, or confused, they display that emotion in their body postures, movement, gestures, and facial expressions. The converse is also true: even when people aren't feeling a specific emotion, if they make facial and body gestures as though they are (for example, frowning and slumping their shoulders), their bodies send that information to their brains and they actually start to feel the emotion that they are physically displaying. We discuss this in more detail in #37 (see page 126).

This emotional contagion also occurs when you are watching a video. If the person in the video is excited and happy, you will start to feel excited and happy, too. This is one reason why video is more powerful than text when you want to get people to take action. And, according to Elizabeth Cohen of West Virginia University, the effect of emotional contagion through video can be amplified when you are watching that video in a group setting.

ANY VISUAL PLUS AUDIO

Talking head videos aren't the only effective communication. Showing pictures while someone talks is also more effective than asking people to read text. Even displaying words on a screen while someone talks is more attention-getting, and communicates more information, than reading alone.

Recently I watched a 20-minute video that consisted of words appearing on the screen in a large font, like a series of slides, while a person talked. It was very effective. I stayed till the end. The words matched what the speaker was saying 99 percent of the time. The visual was just slides with one sentence or phrase in black text on a white background. There were no images. But the speaker's voice was interesting and compelling, as was the content, so I stayed.

THERE ARE OTHER CHOICES

We're stuck in old media: books become e-books, TV becomes online videos, newspapers and magazines become online articles, posters become infographics, presentations become slideshares, lectures become online video courses.

A few pioneers are experimenting with new forms. Scaleofuniverse.com (Figure 29.1) lets people explore an entire universe of information by scrolling and clicking.

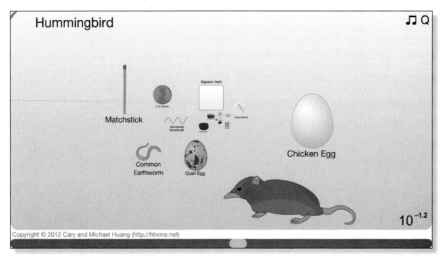

FIGURE 29.1 Scaleofuniverse.com.

Flowingdata.com (Figure 29.2) presents data interactively. The visitor decides how much to explore and what to look at next.

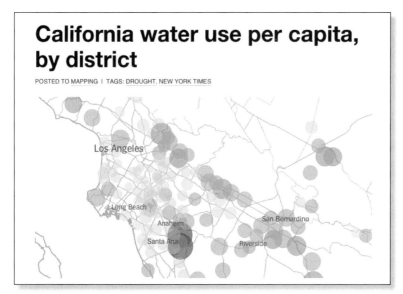

FIGURE 29.2 Flowingdata.com.

It's time to embrace these interactive models in an everyday way rather than simply as novelties. And it's time for designers to come up with the next generation of ways to communicate information.

Takeaways

- ☑ Since video has so many advantages over text, consider video before you decide what and how much text to use in your design.

- ☑ Since audio is just as important—and sometimes more important—than video, consider using a person talking with visuals when you need to communicate.

- ☑ If you're unfamiliar with some of the new interaction maps and interactive data, try them out. Experiment with letting go of old media frameworks and try one of the new interactive frameworks.

- ☑ The world is waiting for even more ways to explore and consume information. If you like to come up with new interaction ideas, spend some time experimenting and let the rest of us know what you're doing.

HOW **PEOPLE** ARE INFLUENCED BY **STORIES**

"Mr and Mrs Dursley, of number four, Privet Drive, were proud to say that they were perfectly normal, thank you very much. They were the last people you'd expect to be involved in anything strange or mysterious, because they just didn't hold with such nonsense."

With that opening sentence from the first Harry Potter book, *Harry Potter and the Philosopher's Stone*, millions of children and adults have been hooked into the story world of Harry Potter.

Stories are like breathing. You breathe between 17,000 and 30,000 times a day. In fact, you breathe so much that you don't realize anymore that you're breathing.

Stories are like that. Stories are important to how people communicate and how the brain works; they're so integral to everyday life that people don't even realize it. If you think you're a designer and not a storyteller, think again. If you want to grab people's attention, get them to respond, and design an experience, you should be telling stories. You probably are already telling stories. But how good are your stories?

30 THE BRAIN IS MORE ACTIVE WITH STORIES

Let's say you're reading a newspaper article I wrote about the impact of the global economy. If you were hooked up to an fMRI machine, it would show that your visual cortex is active, since you're reading, as is Wernicke's area of the brain, where words are processed.

What if you were listening to me give a presentation on the same topic? I'm giving you facts and figures, but not telling a story. The fMRI would again show that Wernicke's area is active, since there are words, and now your auditory cortex would be active as well, because you're listening to me speak.

But what if, during the presentation, I started telling you a story about a family in South America that's being affected by changes in the global economy—a story about the father going to work in a foreign country to earn enough for the family, and the mother having to drive 100 kilometers for health care. What's going on in your brain now? Wernicke's area would be active again, as well as the auditory cortex, but now there would be more activity. If, in my story, I described the sharp smell of the pine forest high in the Andes where this family lives, the olfactory sensory areas of the brain would be active as though you were smelling the forest. If I described the mother driving over rutted, muddy roads, with the vehicle careening from side to side, your motor cortex would be lighting up as though you were driving on a bumpy road. And if I started talking about the devastation the family felt when their young son died before he could get medical treatment, then the empathy areas of the brain would be active.

Stories evoke a simulation of the event. Your brain reacts to the story as if you were *in* the story, and having the experience.

This means that you're literally using more of your brain when you listen to a story. And because you're having a richer brain event, you enjoy the experience more, you understand the information more deeply, and you retain it longer.

AND WITH EMOTIONAL CHEMICALS, TOO

When you listen to a story, your brain releases neurochemicals throughout your body.

If the story is tense, then the hormone cortisol will be released (cortisol modulates stress). If the story is heartwarming, then oxytocin is released (oxytocin makes people feel bonded to others). If the story has a happy ending, then dopamine is released (dopamine makes people feel optimistic and seek action).

STORIES AND YOUR PRODUCT

You may think that, as a designer, stories aren't part of what you do. Writers write stories, or speakers tell stories. But designers don't.

That's a narrow view of design. I used to hear people who design websites say that they weren't responsible for the content of the website—just the design. Or they weren't responsible for picking out the photos, just for preparing and placing them on the page. As a designer, you're active in decisions about the product. You may not have the final say, but you're part of the team. Just as you have to pay attention to and be involved with decisions about interaction, visual design, and content, you need to be involved in decisions about stories, too.

Stories are so important as a medium that if you want to design a compelling product and have people use it, you have to at least influence the use of stories and the way they're told.

If you don't create stories yourself then, at the very least, you can be an advocate for effective stories.

STORIES AND THE DESIGN PROCESS

Even if you think you have nothing to do with stories for the actual product, you *do* have stories when it comes to design. Do you create scenarios? Storyboards? Present your design ideas to your team, stakeholders, or clients? Any design process involves summarizing and explaining how the target audience for a product is going to use that product. These are stories too, so even if you don't do any work on other stories, at least use what you know about stories to sell your design ideas to your team.

Takeaways

☑ When the product you're designing doesn't use stories, or doesn't use them effectively, speak up. If you're not empowered to create good stories, at least alert someone who is.

☑ Look for opportunities to add stories. Whenever you provide information, facts, or data, there's a place in there for a story.

☑ When you're responsible for pictures and graphics, evaluate how you use them. A photo or a series of photos can also tell a story even without words.

☑ When you present your ideas and storyboards to stakeholders or your team, use strong stories to influence others to buy into your design.

31 DRAMATIC ARC STORIES CHANGE BRAIN CHEMICALS

"Ben's dying."

This is the opening line to a video that Paul Zak (author of *The Moral Molecule*) used to research the relationship between stories and brain chemicals.

Note You can watch a short video about Zak's research on storytelling and the dramatic arc here: (https://www.youtube.com/watch?v=q1a7tiA1Qzo).

Zak ran experiments with the video. The video is a true story about a 2-year-old boy who was dying of brain cancer. In the video, Ben's father talks about his son. He says that Ben felt better after his chemotherapy and so was often playing happily, but that he (the father) had a difficult time being joyful even when Ben was, because he knew that Ben would die within a few months as a result of his brain tumor.

Zak found that when people watched the video they experienced two emotions: first, distress, and then later, empathy. He took blood samples before and after people watched the video. He found that when people felt distress they released cortisol, and when they felt empathy they released oxytocin. Zak then gave people a chance to share money with a stranger in the lab or to donate money to a charity that helped children who were ill. In both cases, the more cortisol and oxytocin people had released, the more money they donated.

Zak concluded, "The narrative (story) is changing behavior by changing brain chemistry."

In another experiment, Zak used the same video and added measurements of heart rate, skin conductance, and respiration. He could predict who would give money based on these measurements. (These new measurements allowed him to study people without having to take blood.)

Zak has examined stories in detail. His research shows that stories that follow the traditional "dramatic arc" are the stories that cause the release of the brain chemicals. In his research, Zak repeated the experiment using a different video of Ben and his father. This video showed Ben and his father at the zoo. It did not have a dramatic arc and did not elicit brain chemical release. Zak also found that the story without the dramatic arc did not hold people's attention.

The dramatic arc Zak refers to comes from Gustav Freytag, a nineteenth-century German playwright and novelist. Freytag studied plays and stories from the Greeks and Shakespeare through to stories from his own time. According to Freytag, an effective story is divided into the five parts shown in Figure 31.1.

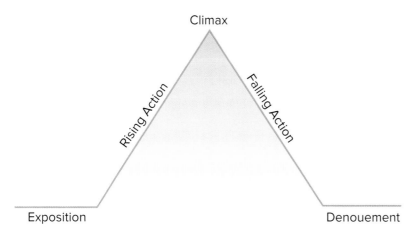

FIGURE 31.1 The dramatic story arc.

1. Exposition—The exposition is the introduction. It sets the time and place, the protagonist or hero, the antagonist or villain, other characters, and the basic conflict of the story.

2. Rising action—The rising action is where the conflict that was introduced during the exposition starts to grow. Tension increases. The initial conflict becomes more complicated.

3. Climax—The climax is the turning point. At the climax, the protagonist has a change of fate. If it's a comedy, then before the climax things were not going well for the protagonist, but after the climax things look up. If it's a tragedy, then the opposite happens. Things get worse for the protagonist. The climax is the highest point in the arc.

4. Falling action—After the climax, it may seem that everything is done, but that's actually not true. This is the last point of suspense. Unexpected things may still happen, so the outcome that the audience thought was set during the climax may or not occur.

5. Denouement—People tend to call the last part of the arc the conclusion, but Freytag called it the denouement. This is a French word referring to an unraveling or untying of a knot. The protagonist either comes out on top (comedy) or the antagonist does (tragedy).

When people watch or hear a story that contains this dramatic arc structure (even if it's a very short story, such as a testimonial on a website), their brains will release cortisol during the rising action and climax, and oxytocin during the falling action and denouement.

COMMON STORIES AND PLOTS

In 1949 Joseph Campbell published *The Hero with a Thousand Faces*. In this book, Campbell traces the myth of the "hero's story." A typical hero's story usually contains the following steps:

1. The hero is living in his ordinary world, but then he receives a message that calls him to adventure and a higher purpose.

2. He often is reluctant to go on the adventure.

3. He has an encounter with someone wise who encourages him to take the first step.

4. He faces some kind of test.

5. He encounters helpers.

6. He has to undergo a harrowing ordeal.

7. He is successful and brings back some kind of treasure.

8. He is transformed and brings the treasure to the rest of the world.

The Harry Potter books contain many examples of the hero's story. Luke Skywalker's storyline in the *Star Wars* movies is an example of a hero's story. (George Lucas specifically cites Joseph Campbell and *The Hero with a Thousand Faces* as critical influences.) Many TED talks are hero stories.

THE SEVEN PLOTS

In addition to the dramatic arc and the hero's story, storytellers often use one of seven basic plots, which may or may not involve a hero:

1. Overcoming a monster—The protagonist has to defeat an antagonist (monster) who is threatening the protagonist's homeland (for example, *Star Wars*).

2. Rags to riches—The protagonist is poor and suddenly becomes wealthy with money, power, and/or a mate. The protagonist loses it all, but then grows as a person and gets the important riches back (for example, *Cinderella*).

3. The quest—The protagonist and friends set out to get something important, face lots of challenges along the way, and eventually are triumphant (for example, *The Lord of the Rings*).

4. Voyage and return—The protagonist goes to a foreign place, makes it through many dangerous situations, and comes back without anything of value, except a personal transformation (for example, *The Chronicles of Narnia*).

5. Comedy—The protagonist is somewhat of a fool and gets into lots of embarrassing situations and near-disasters, but in the end triumphs over all the adversities and finds happiness (for example, *A Midsummer Night's Dream*).

6. Tragedy—There may be a protagonist or an antagonist. He or she ends up with a tragic ending/death. He or she may learn from the troubles encountered along the way, but not enough to be redeemed in this life (for example, *Macbeth*).

7. Rebirth—Instead of a protagonist, there's an antagonist. He or she learns and *is* redeemed over the course of the story (for example, *Beauty and the Beast*).

These common plots resonate with people. When a story follows one of these plots, people can easily understand the story and are more likely to become involved.

Takeaways

☑ When you want people to take an empathetic action, follow the dramatic arc.

☑ Simply creating a video doesn't guarantee that you'll capture your audience's attention. The video needs to follow the dramatic arc or people may not stay engaged.

☑ Use the dramatic arc in your storyboards and when you explain to others how people will use your design.

32 STORIES FOCUS ATTENTION

If you want people to be engaged and pay attention to your design and your message, use a story. And for maximum attention, introduce tension into the story.

In the dramatic arc discussed earlier in this chapter, the second part of the arc (after the exposition) is rising action. The rising action contains tension. When there's tension, people pay attention. The stories that designers use (for example, a story from a customer at a website, or a video) are often short. If the story is short, then you have to build the tension very quickly to grab attention.

As shown in Figure 32.1, tension in a story causes the brain to release cortisol. This makes people pay attention. If people sustain attention long enough, then they begin to identify with the characters in the story. This will lead to oxytocin release, which then leads to empathy.

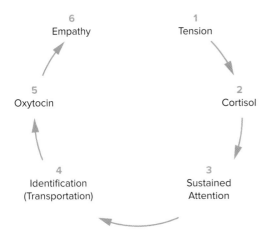

FIGURE 32.1 The attention circle.

People who study stories, or "narratives," call this identification with the characters "transportation."

Transportation is an actual physical reaction. When people start to identify with the characters, they smile when the characters are happy, and cry when the characters are sad. People's brains react as though they themselves were in the story. The shorter the story, the simpler and more clear the main character's actions need to be in order to activate transportation.

TENSION IN STORYBOARDS

Designers often use storyboards to tell the story of a target audience and how that audience interacts with a brand or product. Designers typically present storyboards to stakeholders or clients.

Storyboards are a form of story even though they're not a narrative. They're like a very short graphic novel.

If you want your audience to buy into your plan or design, then treat your storyboard like a story. Build in tension to grab and hold the audience's attention. In the storyboard, show the problem, danger, or hope of the target audience, build the tension quickly, and then resolve it with your design.

Takeaways

☑ When you use a story in your design, build tension quickly, especially if the story is short.

☑ Be clear about who the main character of the story is so that transportation, or identification with the character, is more likely to occur.

☑ Treat your storyboards as actual stories. Use tension so that the people you're presenting the storyboard to will pay attention and will feel empathy for the target audience you're describing with the storyboard.

33 PEOPLE'S SELF-STORIES AFFECT THEIR BEHAVIOR

People have an idea of who they are and what's important to them. They have self-stories that they tell themselves and other people about who they are, why they do what they do, and why they believe what they believe.

People like to be consistent with their self-stories. So if I feel that I'm someone who's very technology savvy, I'll want to stay consistent with that. In fact, it will make me uncomfortable if I come across a situation in which it seems like I'm not technology savvy. I won't like that, because it doesn't fit my self-story. These self-stories have a powerful influence on the decisions people make and the actions they take.

As a designer, you can connect with your audience on a deeper level if you know their self-story. For example, let's say my self-story is that I'm an expert at video equipment. If I come to your website and it seems that the website is for people who are new to video technology, then I may quickly decide that your website is not for me. I will want to stay consistent with my self-story. I'll filter out anything that doesn't fit with my self-story.

One of the reasons that designers research and document personas is to understand the self-stories of the target audience and to be able to design to fit those self-stories. If you know who your target audience is, then you can craft your message to speak to that audience. When you craft the message to speak to that target audience, you're tapping into their self-story.

Let's say you're designing an app to encourage people to sign up for a walk/run event to raise money for a charity. How you promote the event, the wording you use, even the wording on the button that people click on to register for the event all depends on what self-story you're going to tap into. For example, if the target audience's self-story is, "I'm someone who cares about helping people who need it," then you'll want to use messaging about helping people. The button to register might say, "Sign me up to help."

If the target audiences' self-story is, "I'm someone who likes to stay fit," then you'll want to use messaging about staying fit. The button might say, "I'm ready to run the 5K." Shaping the wording of text and buttons to fit a self-story makes it more likely that the person reading it will take action.

Takeaways

☑ Identify the most important self-stories of your target audience so you'll know what messaging will be influential for them.

☑ When you want people to take an action, use messaging and wording that matches an active self-story of your target audience.

34 SMALL STEPS CAN CHANGE SELF-STORIES

If people want to stay consistent with their self-stories, and if they filter out information that doesn't match their self-stories, can you ever get people to change? Can you ever get people to take an action that doesn't fit their self-stories?

The answer is yes, but you have to start small.

A CRACK IN THE SELF-STORY

I used to be a person who didn't like Apple products. I had always used Microsoft Windows products and had little exposure to Apple products. I thought Apple products were for students or graphic designers. That wasn't me. I was more of a computer nerd or a geek than an artist.

My husband used Apple computers at his job (at a newspaper), and he and I would have "Apple/PC" wars. I swore I would "never buy an Apple product." That's a pretty strong self-story.

When MP3 players first came on the market, they were poorly designed and not very usable. Then Apple introduced the iPod. My children really wanted an iPod. But if I bought them an iPod, I was breaking my promise to myself. It would be inconsistent with my self-story.

On the other hand, I wanted to be a fun parent and get my children the latest cool gadget. So I broke with my self-story and bought them each an iPod.

That was a small step, not in alignment with my self-story. But it was small. I could justify it. It caused me a little bit of discomfort, but not too much. When people take a small action that goes against an active self-story, it causes conflict. It has to be a small action, or else people are unlikely to take it. If it's small enough and people take the action, they've now introduced a crack in their self-story.

THE CRACK WIDENS

Now that the children had iPods I began to be frustrated with my MP3 player. Their iPods were cooler and easier to use than my MP3 player. I decided to buy an iPod.

This was a larger step. I wasn't buying this for my children. It was for me. The only reason I was willing to take that step was that I had already taken the first step of buying an Apple product at all. Now buying another iPod was actually consistent with the previous action.

I could still rationalize that this iPod purchase for me didn't mean that I was an Apple person. It was just an iPod. I was still a PC person.

I didn't realize it at the time, but buying that iPod for me widened the crack in my self-story and allowed me to continue taking actions that were now consistent with a new, developing self-story. I was a person who was open to new, cooler gadgets. I was a person who could adjust to the latest "thing." I was a person who bought Apple products.

Without realizing what was happening, I started taking actions consistent with the self-story of someone who buys Apple products. When my phone needed replacing, I bought an iPhone. When my laptop needed replacing, I bought a MacBook Pro. Eventually I bought everything Apple, including, more iPods, iPads, a Mac desktop, and an Apple TV.

I had totally changed my self-story, but it all started with one little action that was inconsistent with the existing self-story.

Interestingly, I think the self-story might change again. I've become enamored with my son's large-size smartphone ("phablet"). But it's an Android product. Am I going to change my self-story to be a Google person instead of an Apple person? My team at work has me using Google docs instead of Mac software. Is that the new crack? I find that I'm not planning on buying an Apple watch. I'm thinking that it's time to upgrade my phone to an Android product.

ENCOURAGING A NEW SELF-STORY

If you want your target audience to take an action that is inconsistent with a strong self-story, get them to take one very small action. Let them use one of your products or services for free, for a short amount of time. That might be enough of a crack to get the self-story to change. Make sure you build in a series of small, easy actions they can take that move them very slowly to a new self-story. Once people make one decision that is inconsistent with one of their self-stories, they will unconsciously feel uncomfortable. They will look for a new self-story to explain their action. By offering a series of small actions, you make it easy for them to transition to a new self-story.

For example, let's say that your company creates SaaS (software as a service) accounting software for small businesses. Your software runs in the cloud. But your target audience has a self-story of "I'm not the kind of person who uses the cloud. I'm not convinced my data is secure that way. If I'm going to use software for my small business, I want it to be on my computer." How will you get them to buy your SaaS product?

You'll need to ask for a small commitment first, and then a series of small commitments. For example, try asking them to download a free trial version of just one of your products first, and then follow that with a reduced rate, three-month subscription for the same product, and after that a free trial of another product. Once they've made one or two small commitments that start to change their self-story, they'll be more likely to continue using the product and to commit to a full year's subscription of more than one product.

Takeaways

- ☑ When you want people to take an action that goes against a self-story, you need to first get them to commit to something small. After that, they'll be more likely to take the next action, since they want their self-stories to be consistent.

- ☑ When you introduce a small crack in an existing self-story, you can change the self-story over time.

- ☑ Plan for a series of small steps of increasing commitment to continue to widen the crack until a new self-story emerges.

---

35 A PUBLIC COMMITMENT LEADS TO STRONGER SELF-STORIES

When people make a public commitment to a product, service, idea, or brand, their self-story about that product, service, idea, or brand becomes stronger. For example, let's say that Maryanne creates custom bowties for weddings and sells her bowties on Etsy. She has a self-story that she is an arts and crafts person, not really a business or marketing person.

But then she watches a short video about the XYZ email marketing service, which claims that when you create an email campaign for potential customers, you can greatly increase your sales. Maryanne wonders if she could increase her sales this way.

The XYZ company offers a free 30-day trial, so she decides to try it out. That's a slight shift in Maryanne's self-story. She can't really say that she's not a business or marketing person if she uses an email marketing service. Maybe she's an arts and crafts person who is also savvy about marketing. If she signs up for the trial and doesn't tell anyone, then the shift in her self-story might stay very small.

But what if she not only signs up for the free trial, but she clicks the "Share" button and shares on her Facebook page that she has signed up for the XYZ email marketing service. That's a form of a public commitment. Unconsciously this will shift her self-story more. The public commitment about the action makes the effect of the action on her self-story stronger than if there were no public commitment.

Taking an action that no one else knows about results in less commitment and will lead to less long-term self-story change than an action that others see.

SURVEYS, REVIEWS, AND TESTIMONIALS

If people have made any commitment at all to your organization, company, product, or service, you can strengthen the commitment and the self-story they have about being committed customers by asking them to make a more public show of support.

As an example, let's say that you work for a hotel chain. When customers stay at the hotel, you send them an email with a link to an online survey about their stay. This survey is a form of public commitment. If they rate your hotel well, then they've made a public commitment that they are a supporter. Be sure to ask how likely they'd be to stay at your hotel again. A survey can be a way for you to get data and feedback about your products and services, but it's also a way to get people to publicly commit. Even if you're the only one who sees the survey result, when people fill out the survey form they will feel that they have made a public commitment, and this will strengthen their self-story that they are a fan of your brand.

You can even send a survey to people who are not yet your customers. If you ask them about their perceptions of your organization, products, or services, and they give positive responses, then they've just committed publicly and will be more open to dealing with you in the future.

The more public people's commitment, the more it will strengthen their self-story—and the more it will affect their current and future behavior. Completing an anonymous survey is better than no commitment at all, but giving a testimonial or recommendation, or writing a review that's posted online, is an even stronger show of commitment.

When people give a recommendation, testimonial, or a written review, they're strengthening a self-story that says, "I am a person who believes in this product," or "I am a person who donates to this organization," or "I am a person who buys from this company."

Reviews act on others as a form of social validation, but they also act on the self as a form of commitment. If people write a positive review, they'll want to stay consistent, and that means they'll take more action to interact with the site, the company, the organization. If you want to build commitment to your brand, your company, or a product, then make sure you give your audience the opportunity to write a review.

 Don't pay people to commit

If you pay people to write a review, testimonial, or respond to a survey, it won't change their self-story. Instead of a self-story of "I am someone who believes in this product," it will be "I'm someone who says I believe in order to get a reward." Rewards (extrinsic motivation) interfere with self-story change (intrinsic motivation).

A reward may get people to take one action, but it won't strengthen their self-story and it won't lead to future action without more reward.

Takeaways

- ☑ Ask people to fill out surveys or write reviews and testimonials. These forms of public commitment will strengthen their self-stories about your brand, product, or service.

- ☑ Don't pay or reward people for making public commitments. Extrinsic motivation (rewards) interferes with intrinsic motivation and will weaken the self-story.

36 CHANGE THE STORY AND YOU WILL CHANGE THE BEHAVIOR

In his book *Redirect: The Surprising New Science of Psychological Change*, Timothy Wilson describes a large body of impressive research on how stories can cause long-term behavior change. Wilson has people rewrite a self-story. He calls this technique "story-editing." Story-editing has been used to help people with post-traumatic stress disorder and teens at risk. The technique of story-editing is so simple that it doesn't seem possible that it could cause such deep and profound change.

When people write a new story that describes who they are, why they behave as they do, and how they relate to others, they will, consciously and unconsciously, start to make decisions and act in ways that are consistent with that story.

But what if you can't get someone to stop, think, and write out a new story? Does that mean that you can't use the powerful effect of stories? Luckily, the answer is no. Even if you can't get people to sit down and write out a new story, you can provide a story for them, and that's almost as good.

Wilson explains how he used story-prompting to help college students stay in school, get better grades, and work harder in their courses. He identified first-year college students who were not doing well. These students were in what he calls a "self-defeating cycle." The students were getting low grades on one or more tests, and had started thinking things like, "I'm in over my head," or "Maybe I don't belong at this college," or "I'm not smart enough." These thoughts created a new story that resulted in behavior that fit, such as not studying and skipping classes. This, of course, resulted in more low grades, reaffirming the story that the students couldn't be successful. Wilson contrasts this with students who might also get a poor grade, but instead of believing the "I'm not smart enough" story, they believe a more hopeful story, such as "This course is harder than I thought it would be," or "I guess my high school work didn't prepare me well enough for this class," or "I'm going to have to work harder, study more, maybe get a tutor." These students' behavior would lead to more studying and getting more help, and therefore better grades.

Wilson's question was whether he could prompt a new story for the "self-defeating" students, even without having them explicitly write a new story themselves. Was there anything he could do to help them switch to a story that was more like the students who reacted to the poor grade by working harder?

Wilson had the students participate in an experiment. They thought they were being asked to take a survey of first-year students' attitudes about college life. Wilson told them that they'd see the results from earlier surveys of older students, so they would know what kind of questions would be on their survey. In actuality, Wilson was showing them the previous survey results in order to prompt them with a new story.

The participants then saw the survey results of these older students that showed that many of the students had problems with grades during their first year, but that their grades improved over time. The participants read statements such as "67 percent said their freshman grades were lower than they had anticipated; 62 percent of the students said their GPA had improved significantly from the first semester of their freshman year to their upper-class years." (This data was true, from actual earlier surveys.) To make sure that the new "story" was clear, the participants also watched video interviews of four older students who gave the same messages. The students in the videos talked about their majors, their hometowns, and career plans and then talked about their GPAs for the first semester of their first year, the second semester of the first year, and the most recent completed semester. All the students in the video interviews talked about their grades steadily increasing over time.

Altogether the participants spent 30 minutes hearing from other students who had problems with low grades, but then improved their grades. Wilson didn't do anything else. He didn't counsel them, teach them study habits, or give them any other help. The participants didn't know that the purpose of the study was to improve their grades. What Wilson hoped was that he had prompted a new story, even if the participants were unaware of it. He hoped to prompt a story such as, "Maybe it's not hopeless. Maybe I'm like those other students. They tried harder and were able to raise their grades."

The story-prompting worked. Wilson reports that the participants achieved better grades in the following year than a randomly assigned control group who did not get the story prompting. The participants were also less likely to drop out of college. Imagine: 30 minutes of reading and watching videos about other people's stories resulted in students working harder, improving their grades, and staying in school.

LET PEOPLE DISCOVER A NEW STORY

Wilson doesn't discuss in his book whether there's a difference between telling people a new story versus letting them "discover" the story on their own. My sense is that the latter is better. The key is that people have to change their own story. If you just give them another story and say, "Here's the story you have and here's the story you should have," it may not have the same impact as letting them discover a new story for themselves and compare it to a story they may not even realize they have. With story-prompting, it's more effective to tell them a story about someone else and let them draw the parallels. Sometimes less is more!

Takeaways

☑ When you want people to take an action, you first need to understand any current self-story that might prevent them from taking the action.

☑ Once you know the current self-story that's preventing them from taking action, craft a new story and then expose them to it.

☑ Use audio, video, or narratives of people telling their stories to effectively influence your target audience to adopt a new story.

HOW **PEOPLE** RELATE TO OTHER **PEOPLE** AND TO **TECHNOLOGY**

Humans are social animals and our behavior is (largely unconsciously) shaped by the desire and instinct to be with other people. We also transfer this social connection to the technologies we interact with. If you design for social interaction, your goal is to design an interface and interaction that people will find compelling. And whether you know it or not, if you're a designer, then designing for robots and artificial intelligence machines that interact with people is likely part of your future.

37 EMOTIONS ARE CONTAGIOUS

I recently went to an improv theater performance. I'd had a busy week, and it was fairly late at night. I was tired and not that excited to be there. In fact, I'd been thinking of not going at all.

As the room began to fill up before the performance started, I noticed that almost everyone there seemed happy and excited. There was a buzz in the room. I found myself waking up, and feeling happy and excited too.

Research has long shown that emotions are contagious. James Fowler (2008) wrote about the spread of happiness over the course of 20 years in one community. There were happy and unhappy groups of people in the network. Happiness extended up to three degrees of separation. People who were surrounded by happy people were more likely to become happy in the future. The statistical analysis showed that this was not just because happy people tended to interact with other happy people, but because people were more likely to become happy when they were around happy people. Even physical distance was important: those who had a happy friend within a mile were 25 percent more likely to become happy themselves. Those with a happy next-door neighbor had a 34 percent greater probability of becoming happier.

And it's not only happiness that's contagious. A 1985 study by M. J. Howes showed that people without depression who roomed with someone who suffered from even mild depression would themselves become depressed over time.

MIMICRY AND EMOTIONS

In the Fowler study, the effects of emotional contagion were seen in people who knew each other over time and were in physical proximity. What about the emotional contagion of strangers? Or people in a video?

Amy Cuddy of the Harvard Business School researches how taking certain postures can cause neurochemical changes in the brain. If you're feeling sad, you frown, hang your head, and contract your body. What you may not realize is that the opposite is also true. Even if you're not sad, if you frown, hang your head, and contract your body, then your body will release neurochemicals that actually make you feel sad. The same is true for other bodily postures and feelings. For example, opening the body with your arms and legs leads to feeling confident and powerful.

One theory about why emotions are contagious is that people tend to mimic the bodily postures of those around them, or of those they see in a video. This, in turn, makes them start to feel the feelings of the people around them, even strangers or people in a video.

We now know that people are affected by the emotional states of other people even in a matter of seconds. Facial expressions are particularly contagious, even through watching a video.

FLAWS IN THE FACEBOOK CONTAGION STUDY

In 2014, Adam Kramer published the results of his 2012 Facebook study, in which he and his team manipulated the Facebook feeds of over 600,000 people to see whether including or eliminating certain posts would affect the subsequent postings. The results were written about in the press as showing emotional contagion through social media. The study has sparked some controversy, including a question about informed consent, as well as concerns about flawed methodologies and measuring tools. (See John Grohol's article on PsychCentral: http://psychcentral.com/blog/archives/2014/06/23/emotional-contagion-on-facebook-more-like-bad-research-methods/). It wouldn't surprise me if there were some amount of emotional contagion through social media, but as I write this I haven't seen research to prove that yet.

Takeaways

☑ When you want to make people feel a particular emotion, concentrate not only on an individual, but on the social group.

☑ When you want people to feel a certain way (happy, excited, concerned, worried), show them photos or videos of people who are displaying that same emotion in their faces and body posture.

38 PEOPLE DON'T LIKE VIDEO ADS

Companies spend a lot of money on video marketing and video advertising, so it's not surprising that there's a significant body of research on these subjects. Thales Teixeira from Harvard Business School is one of the people conducting research on video ads.

People are inundated with advertising: TV ads, billboards on the road, ads at the start of YouTube videos. Teixeira's research (2012) shows that in general, people do not like ads. Even when they like a particular video ad, in general, people don't like ads.

In the past, people had few choices when it came to ads. When an ad appeared on TV, they could change the station or turn off the TV.

Now it's sometimes possible to bypass ads. For example, some people may have technology that lets them skip an ad on a recording, or skip an ad on YouTube.

Because people don't like ads, and because they now can often avoid them, ad designers have to be more savvy. Messaging has to come earlier, and the ads themselves have to grab and hold people's attention (more on this later in this chapter).

PEOPLE DON'T LIKE BRAND LOGOS

In his research, Teixeira notes that people especially dislike seeing a lot of brand logos in ads. The more prominent a brand logo is, the more likely people are to skip the ad. This is true even for brands they like. So some advertisers are doing what's called "brand pulsing": placing their brand logo as unobtrusively as possible throughout the ad.

Takeaways

☑ Put the main message at the beginning of the ad, not at the end.

☑ Since people don't like ads, don't remind them they're viewing an ad by placing the brand icon or logo prominently at the beginning.

☑ Don't use the logo a lot. Instead, weave the logo subtly and infrequently into the storyline of the ad.

---

39 JOY AND SURPRISE GRAB AND HOLD ATTENTION IN VIDEO ADS

Teixeira's research shows that joy and surprise are the emotions that keep people watching a video ad. Because people don't like ads and want to skip them, ads that stimulate both joy and surprise early on are the ones that grab and hold attention best.

Teixeira used software that analyzes facial expressions to research the influence of emotions on ad watching. The researchers collected data every 250 milliseconds while people watched video ads. Each participant saw 28 video ads. Fourteen of them had emotional content and 14 were neutral. The neutral ads were interspersed with the emotional ads.

Half of the emotional ads were designed to evoke joy, measured with smiles and laughter, and the other half to evoke surprise, measured with raised eyebrows and an open mouth. The ads varied. Some were for beverages, some for phones, some for financial services, and so on. Some were for well-known brands and others for lesser-known brands.

Participants could either watch each ad to the end, "zap" to the next ad, or click on a link that would take them to the ad brand's web page. (These were one-page mock-up websites that were kept short and simple).

The researchers found the following results:

- Both joy and surprise grabbed the attention of the participants, but surprise grabbed attention more than joy, and joy was better than surprise in keeping people viewing longer.

- The best strategy for grabbing attention was what the researchers called a "peak and stable trajectory"—heighten the emotion and then leave it high.

- However, the best strategy to retain viewers was a "peak-valley-peak" strategy—heighten emotion, then let it die down, then bring it back up again, and continue alternating (an emotional rollercoaster).

Takeaways

☑ To grab attention in a video ad, put something surprising at the beginning of the ad.

☑ To retain attention during a video ad, use content that evokes joy.

☑ To sustain attention, vary the amount of joy and surprise or any other emotions, so that people are having an emotionally up-and-down experience.

40 SURPRISE, BUT NOT SHOCK, ENCOURAGES SHARING

In his book *Contagious*, Jonah Berger talks about *New York Times* online articles that get shared. Articles that had elicited strong emotion, whether positive or negative, were shared the most. Jennifer Aaker talks about emotion and passion as being components of what makes messages go viral in her book *The Dragonfly Effect*.

In his research, Teixeira found that people can like an online video and yet not share it. He notes that surprise makes it more likely that people will share an online video, but not if the surprise goes too far and becomes shock.

Watching something that is so surprising that it is shocking will sustain attention, but people don't like to share online videos that are shocking. As examples, Teixeira cites two Bud Light ads. In one ad, people in an office start swearing when they realize that every time someone in the office swears, money is added to a "swear jar." When the jar is full of money, the office manager buys a case of Bud Light beer for everyone to share. That video is surprising, but not shocking, and people tend to share it with others.

In contrast, another Bud Light ad, using the same cast and the same office environment, shows the office staff donating used clothing for a charity. Every time someone donates an article of clothing, he or she gets a Bud Light beer. In the video there are scenes in the office of people taking off more and more clothing until they are essentially naked (with private parts blacked out in the video). This video is surprising, but it goes beyond surprise to shock. It sustained attention, but was not shared as much as the other video that was surprising without being shocking.

EXTROVERSION, EGOCENTRICITY, AND SHARING

Teixeira's research shows that even when a video ad is surprising and not shocking, only a subset of people will share it. Who is the sharing subgroup? Extroverts share more than introverts. And people who are egocentric share more than those who are not.

Teixeira's hypothesis is that egocentric people share in order to increase their social status. They are sharing to show others how savvy they are.

He suggests that if you want your content to go viral, figure out how to find the egocentric extroverts, for example, people who already share a lot on social media.

Takeaways

- ☑ When you want your content to go viral, include strong emotional content, especially content that produces positive emotions.

- ☑ When you want your content to go viral, make sure the material is surprising, but not shocking.

- ☑ When you want your content to go viral, target people who are extroverts and/or egocentric. Look for people who are already active on social media.

41 OXYTOCIN IS THE BONDING CHEMICAL

Singing and theater are favorite hobbies of mine. At various points in my life I have sung in a choir, played in concert bands, played in a marching band, played and sang in jazz ensembles, and acted and sang in musical theater productions. It's great fun on many levels, but one of the things that makes it the most fun is the feeling of camaraderie that comes from making music with others.

I wasn't surprised, then, to find out that a neurochemical is released in the brain when people engage in synchronous activity with others, for example, singing, playing a musical instrument, chanting, drumming, or dancing. That neurochemical is oxytocin.

THE BONDING CHEMICAL

In *The Moral Molecule,* Paul Zak discusses research showing that when people bond through group activity, oxytocin levels are elevated. This explains why doing group activities bonds the group.

Oxytocin is released by the posterior lobe of the pituitary gland. Oxytocin has several effects:

- Women release oxytocin during labor. Oxytocin produces the contractions that start the birthing process.

- Women also release oxytocin when they nurse their babies.

- Oxytocin reduces inflammation and helps heal wounds. This is one of the reasons why having a strong social network keeps you healthy—the bonding releases oxytocin and the oxytocin reduces inflammation.

- Oxytocin makes people feel content, calm, and secure. It also decreases anxiety.

- People are more likely to trust someone after oxytocin is released.

Whenever oxytocin is released, people feel love, tenderness, empathy, and trust. They feel a sense of belonging and connectedness. People who are incapable of releasing oxytocin have a tendency to become sociopathic, psychopathic, or narcissistic.

When you hug someone or stroke a dog, your body releases oxytocin. In fact, research shows that not only does your oxytocin level go up, but so does that of the dog.

Think of oxytocin as the tribal hormone. Some research shows that oxytocin is related to a feeling of connectedness to one's group or tribe, and suspicion of "others" outside the group or tribe.

Heart rates in sync

In addition to releasing oxytocin, group musical and rhythmic activity has other effects. When people sing together, their breathing and heartbeats sync up. Björn Vickhoff (2013) attached pulse monitors to the ears of choir singers. When the choir began to sing, their heart rates slowed down, probably due to the regularities in breathing that singing requires. The slower heart rates didn't surprise Vickhoff, but the syncing of the heart rates did.

SYNCHRONOUS BEHAVIOR AND COOPERATION

Scott Wiltermuth and Chip Heath (2009) conducted a series of studies to see whether, and how, synchronous behavior affects how people cooperate. They tested combinations of walking in step, not walking in step, singing together, and other movements with groups of participants.

Synchronous activities are actions that people take together, where everyone is doing the same thing at the same time in physical proximity to one another. Dancing, tai chi, yoga, singing, clapping, and chanting in time are all examples of synchronous activity.

The researchers found that people who engaged in synchronous activities were more cooperative in completing subsequent tasks, and more willing to make personal sacrifices to benefit the group.

Wiltermuth and Heath's research also showed that people don't have to feel good about the group, or the group activity, in order to be more cooperative. The mere act of doing the synchronous activity seemed to strengthen social attachment among the group members.

Do people need synchronous activity to be happy?

In his 2008 article "Hive Psychology, Happiness, and Public Policy," Jonathan Haidt goes so far as to say that because synchronous activity promotes bonding, it helps the survival of the group. He believes that there's a certain type of happiness that humans can achieve only by engaging in synchronous activity.

DESIGNING FOR SYNCHRONOUS INTERACTIONS

As a designer, you probably spend most of your time designing interactions that are asynchronous—*not* synchronous. If you're designing a website or software, there's a high probability that each member of your target audience will be using that application on his own, without singing, drumming, or chanting!

But there may be opportunities for synchronous behavior. If you're creating a video, you could include a well-known song with lyrics that people will be encouraged to sing along with. If you have a choice about how to convey information, you could choose a more synchronous way, for example, have people meet via video conference rather than sending emails or tracking documents in a workflow app.

Takeaways

☑ Look for opportunities to have your target audience do something at the same time. For example, meeting via video conference is better than not meeting at all.

☑ Look for opportunities to have your target audience do something synchronous with you and your brand. Even including a catchy song that they can sing along to will produce a small amount of bonding.

☑ Look for opportunities to have your design team bond together.

42 WHEN PEOPLE FEEL CONNECTED, THEY WORK HARDER

Gregory Walton is a professor at Stanford who has studied the important effects of belonging on behavior. In one of his experiments, Walton (2012) found that when college students believed they shared a birthday with another student, they were more motivated to complete a task with that student and performed better on the task than if they were not told about any connection. He found the same effect with 4- and 5-year-olds.

In another experiment with Walton, David Cwir (2011) had people who were part of the experiment jog in place in pairs, raising their heart rate. Participants who felt they were socially connected to their running partner (for example, were told they had the same birthday) had an increase in their heart rate as the other person's heart rate increased from jogging. They also rated the other person as being more connected to them than people who were not told they had the same birthday.

Cwir and Walton concluded that it's easy for people to take on the goals, motivations, emotions, and even physical reactions of people whom they feel even minimally connected to.

THE SOCIAL FACILITATION EFFECT

When people *think* they're working together, they work better and longer, and enjoy it more. Research on the "social facilitation effect" goes all the way back to 1920. Floyd Allport (1920) conducted a series of experiments with male college students. In some situations, students worked on word association or writing tasks in a room alone; in other situations, they worked in a group, although all the work was done individually. Allport controlled carefully for things like light and noise.

Here's what he found:

- People working in a group came up with ideas faster (from 66 percent to up to 93 percent faster) than people working alone.

- People working in a group came up with more ideas than people working alone.

- Most individuals did better in the group settings, but a few people who were, in Allport's words, "nervous and excitable," showed no difference or a slight decrease when they were with the group.

Priyanka Carr and Gregory Walton (2014) did a more recent series of experiments where they implied that people were working together, when actually everyone was working alone.

In the psychologically together group, participants were told that the study investigated how people work on puzzles together and that they and the other participants would each work on a puzzle called the "map puzzle."

Participants in this together group were told that, after working on the puzzle for several minutes, they would either be asked to write a tip for another person working on the puzzle, or they would receive a tip from another participant also working on the map puzzle.

The experimenter explained the puzzle, told the participant to take as much or as little time as they wanted on the puzzle, and then left the room.

A few minutes later the experimenter came back and gave the participant a tip that said, "Here's a tip one of the other participants here today wrote for you to help you as you work on the puzzle." The tip was actually from the experimenter, but was presented as though it was from another participant. It had a "To" line with the participant's first name, and a "From" line with the supposed first name of another participant.

In the psychologically separate group, the experimenter told participants that the research investigated how people work on puzzles and that they would work on a puzzle called the "map puzzle." The instructions implied that the other participants in the study were working on the same puzzle, but no mention was made of working together.

Participants in this separate group were told that, after working on the puzzle for several minutes, they would either be asked to write a tip for or would receive a tip from the experimenter about the puzzle. When they received a tip it said, "Here's a tip we wrote for you to help you as you work on the puzzle" and it was presented as being from the experimenter. Instead of "To" and "From," there was a "For" line with the participant's first name. Otherwise the instructions were the same as for the psychologically together group.

The participants in the together group worked longer on the puzzle, rated the puzzle as being more enjoyable, performed better, and were more likely to choose to work on a related task one to two weeks later than those in the separate group.

Takeaways

☑ When you want your target audience to feel connected to your brand or product, point out anything that you share in common with them.

☑ When you're designing in a team, make sure to point out things that the team members have in common, even if they seem small and superficial.

☑ When you're designing in a team, monitor your language. Use words that imply that people are working together ("we," "team," "together").

43 DEVICES WITH ALERTS LOWER COGNITIVE PERFORMANCE

There's a lot of research about how talking or texting on a cell phone is distracting and leads to lower performance on cognitive (thinking) tasks, but research by Bill Thornton (2014) shows that people don't even have to be *using* the cell phone for it to have an effect. Just having the cell phone nearby can lower performance on cognitive tasks. It's likely that the mere presence of the cell phone distracts people enough that they don't concentrate as well.

PAVLOVIAN CONDITIONED RESPONSES

In the early 1900s, Ivan Pavlov was studying digestion in dogs. He fed them meat and measured the amount of saliva they produced. He was surprised to discover that the dogs started salivating as soon as they saw the meat, and before they started eating it. But the bigger surprise was that, before too long, the dogs would salivate when they heard the boots of the caretaker coming to feed them, or when they heard the sound of a bell over the door when the caretaker walked into the building. Pavlov posited that the dogs had learned a conditioned response (salivating) to the stimulus of the footsteps or bell.

People also easily learn conditioned responses—their response to buzzing, blinking, chirping, flashing, and now, with wearables, nudging, is to look at or reach for the device. Part of the human brain is always on "alert" for the stimulus, which likely takes just enough brain power away from other tasks for performance to suffer, even if only a little bit.

People easily develop automatic, conditioned responses to auditory and visual cues, especially if those cues are short and unpredictable. And smartphones provide endless unpredictable, short, auditory and visual cues. You don't know when you'll get a text or call, so it's unpredictable. When you do get a text or a call or your phone rings, chirps, or buzzes, or a message shows on the screen, there's an auditory and visual cue. And the messages are short—all features that prompt a conditioned and automatic response.

Takeaways

☑ When you want people to concentrate or perform better on a task that requires thinking, make sure it's easy for them to turn off alerts in your product, software, or app.

☑ Rethink the need for alerts and notifications. Make it easy for people to find information when they want it and use that approach instead of relying on auditory or visual alerts.

☑ If you must have alerts, consider making the default such that alerts are turned off.

44 CELL PHONES NEARBY NEGATIVELY AFFECT PERSON-TO-PERSON COMMUNICATION

Imagine that you're sitting in a restaurant with a friend and he takes his smartphone out of his pocket, turns off the sound, and puts it off to the side, face down, on the table. He doesn't touch it all through the meal you have together. He doesn't look at it, text with it, or even glance at it. Can the mere presence of the phone change your relationship with him?

The answer is yes, and not for the better!

Andrew Przybylski and Netta Weinstein (2013) studied how the presence of a cell phone affects the way people communicate with each other.

The idea from social psychologists is this: Because people use their mobile devices to stay connected with people who are not in close proximity, it's easy to build a conditioned response to the device and think of it as "everyone else." When the device, for example, a smartphone, is sitting on the table at the restaurant, it is representing the rest of its owner's social network. In a way, his whole social network is actually at the restaurant.

The smartphone will therefore trigger thinking about other people and other events outside the immediate context, which will in turn divert attention away from the experiences that are occurring at the particular time and place.

Some of this may occur consciously, but some of this "not being present" occurs unconsciously. Social psychologists, including Przybylski and Weinstein, theorize that these devices can, therefore, have a negative impact on person-to-person relationships.

To research the idea, they ran two experiments. In the first experiment people who did not know each other were assigned to pairs, asked to leave all their personal belongings outside the room, and then told to "Discuss an interesting event that occurred to you over the past month," for 10 minutes. For half of the pairs, there was a mobile phone (not belonging to either person) on top of a book. The book was on a nearby desk, but not in the direct visual field of the participants. The other half of the pairs had the same room setup, but without a mobile phone.

After the 10-minute discussion, each participant individually filled out forms to measure things such as relationship quality, closeness, and positive affect.

The pairs that had been in the room with the mobile phone felt less close to each other, and rated the relationship lower than the pairs in a room without a cell phone present.

In the second experiment, some of the pairs were instructed to discuss their "thoughts and feelings about plastic holiday trees" (casual condition). Other pairs were instructed to discuss "the most meaningful events of the past year" (meaningful condition). The surveys were the same as in the first experiment, except some new surveys were added to measure trust and empathy.

When the mobile phone was in the room participants gave lower ratings on all the measures, including the new trust and empathy measures. But this effect was stronger in the meaningful condition pairs than the casual condition pairs.

The researchers concluded that simply placing the cell phone in the room interfered with the formation of a new relationship, and that the negative effect of the cell phone was stronger during a meaningful conversation.

ESTABLISHING PROJECT RELATIONSHIPS

Although this research may not directly apply to the designs you create, it certainly can apply any time you meet with clients, stakeholders, users, or your own team. Think about all the meetings you have. Sometimes people ask the group to turn off cell phones, usually to avoid interruptions or distractions. You may want to not only have people turn off their phones, but also put them away. This will make it easier to establish and/or deepen the project relationships as well as establish and increase trust.

Takeaways

- ☑ When you're establishing a new relationship with someone, don't have a cell phone in view.

- ☑ When you're trying to deepen an interpersonal relationship or get someone to trust you, don't have a cell phone in view.

- ☑ When you're in a meeting, model the behavior by not only turning off your cell phone, but actually putting it out of view.

- ☑ When you're running a meeting, ask everyone to turn off their cell phones and put them out of view.

45 PEOPLE TRUST MACHINES THAT HAVE SOME HUMAN-LIKE CHARACTERISTICS

If you haven't been part of a design project that involves robots, robotics, or autonomous vehicles, just wait. Unless you're about to retire, it's likely that you'll be involved in some kind of robot design during your career.

So how do you design interactions between people and machines when the machines are now doing tasks that humans used to do? What do people expect from these machines, and how do people react to their design?

As I write this book, Google's self-driving car is being tested. An article in the *Washington Post* reminds us that John Deere has been selling autonomous tractors for a while now (http://www.washingtonpost.com/blogs/the-switch/wp/2015/06/22/google-didnt-lead-the-self-driving-vehicle-revolution-john-deere-did/?tid=magnet).

Whether it's a tractor, a car, a vacuum cleaner, or a sociable robot, machines that people interact with (even more than they do with their computers and smartphones) have arrived. And as a designer, you'll be creating the interfaces for them.

ANTHROPOMORPHISM AND TRUST

The Google car has no pedals for the gas or brakes. The human doesn't steer. All the human does is start the car (and stop it in an emergency). Adam Waytz, Joy Heafner, and Nicholas Epley (2014) wanted to know if giving machines more human-like qualities would increase the amount of trust that people had in the machine. They tested how anthropomorphism would affect trust. They define anthropomorphism as:

> a process of inductive inference whereby people attribute to nonhumans distinctively human characteristics, particularly the capacity for rational thought (agency) and conscious feeling (experience)

The researchers' idea was that if a machine were seen to be more human, then it would be seen to be more thoughtful, more mindful. They hypothesized that people trust people who are more thoughtful, and so they would trust machines that seem more thoughtful, too. Thoughtfulness is something that people attribute to other people. If people think an autonomous car or a robot reading x-rays is just a "mindless" machine, they won't trust it as much. Conversely, if the machine seems to be "thinking" more like a human, then people will think the machine will be better able to control its own actions—it's being mindful, not mindless.

In their experiment, the researchers used a driving simulator and engineered the simulation so that there was an accident in which participants were struck by an oncoming car. The simulation made it obvious that the accident was caused by a human driver in the other car.

Participants were assigned to either a normal, agentic, or anthropomorphic condition:

- In the normal condition, the participants were driving, with no automatic features from the car.

- In the agentic condition, the participants drove an autonomous car. The car controlled its own steering and speed. Participants in this condition were told what was going to happen, and how and when to use the autonomous features.

- In the anthropomorphic condition, the participants drove the same autonomous car, but in addition to being told what was going to happen and how to use the autonomous features, the experimenter referred to the car with the name Iris, and referred to the car as a "she." A human voice was also attributed to the car. The voice spoke at certain times during the simulation, and gave the instructions.

Participants in the agentic and anthropomorphic conditions first drove on a practice course to try out the autonomous features. Then everyone in all the conditions drove the course.

Participants in the anthropomorphic condition blamed their car less for the accident than did those in the normal or agentic conditions. Participants in the anthropomorphic group rated the car as having more human-like mental capacities than people in the agentic group. They trusted their car more, and showed a more relaxed heart rate when the "accident" occurred.

BEWARE OF THE UNCANNY VALLEY

Some humanizing of a machine makes people more willing to trust it, but how far does that go?

Anthropomorphizing entails acting like a human, but not necessarily looking like one. People who design robots have to be careful about what's called "the uncanny valley."

The uncanny valley is the idea that as things, particularly robots and animated characters, become more realistic, they eventually hit a point where people find them creepy and nonhuman. This is due to small inconsistencies, for example, the skin texture or the reflection in the eyes may seem a bit off. People unconsciously notice these things because these are attributes that they observe daily in interactions with others.

The uncanny valley theory originated from Masahiro Mori, while working with robotics in the 1970s. An article of his from the 1970s was recently translated into English (2012).

Mori's theory was that people's reactions to robots range from lack of connection to comfort and connection to alienation, depending on how lifelike the robot is. If the robot is a little bit like a person, then people will feel empathy and connection. But if it becomes very human-like without getting past the "not quite human" feeling, then people's reaction turns to revulsion. Figure 45.1 shows a graph of the relationship between people's comfort level with the robot or machine compared to the degree of human-likeness. The place where the comfort level dips dramatically is the uncanny valley.

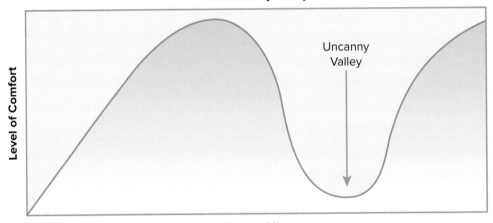

FIGURE 45.1   The uncanny valley.

Research by Christine Looser (2010) shows that it is the deadness of the eyes that makes people feel that the robot is not human and that it is creepy.

The uncanny valley exists for robots, machines, and animated characters.

Note   Japan's National Museum of Emerging Science and Innovation had an exhibition called Android: What Is Human? that explored the uncanny valley. The exhibition included several human-looking robot newscasters. Here are some articles with videos of the robots and the exhibition:

http://www.engadget.com/2014/06/12/home-robot-pepper/

http://www.engadget.com/2014/06/25/androids-humanoid-robots-newscaster/

Takeaways

☑ When you design an interface for a machine that's doing tasks that humans usually do, build in some human-like (anthropomorphic) characteristics.

☑ Don't design a machine or animation that looks and acts exactly like a human unless you can take it all the way.

46 PEOPLE CAN FEEL EMPATHY FOR MACHINES

Trusting your autonomous car or tractor is not the same thing as having a social relationship with it or caring about it.

People's interactions with machines are moving beyond anthropomorphism and trust. People are now encountering situations in which they're developing social relationships with machines and robots.

Kate Darling is a research specialist at the Media Lab. She conducts research with a dinosaur toy called Pleo that looks like a baby dinosaur. Darling has people interact with Pleo first on their own, and then she asks them to do hurtful things to Pleo: hitting him, holding him upside down, holding him by the neck, and so on.

Pleo makes distressing noises when people do these things to him. Darling finds that people don't like to hurt the toy, even though they know it's not alive and can't feel what is being done to it.

Astrid Rosenthal-von der Pütten (2013) used an fMRI machine to study empathy toward machines. She had people watch videos. Sometimes the video showed a person being treated roughly or harmed, and sometimes it was the Pleo toy being hurt.

The same areas of the brain were active when people saw the person or the Pleo being treated poorly.

 Confiding in an anthropomorphic robot

BlabDroid is a small, simple-looking robot that asks questions (in a voice that sounds like a small boy), and films the interaction. BlabDroid tells you what button to press to get started, asks questions, and then films the interaction. The questions include:

"If there was no money, and no law, what would be the first thing you would do?"

"What is the last risk you took?"

"Who do you love most in the world?"

"When do you feel the most nervous?"

"What are you the most proud of?"

"If you died tomorrow, what would you regret the most?"

You can watch BlabDroid in action at https://www.youtube.com/watch?v=PuhpoRnqlu0.

A creation of Alexander Reben, BlabDroid is remarkable for eliciting open and vulnerable responses from the people it talks to. And BlabDroid is just a box made out of cardboard with a smile on it.

Takeaways

☑ When you're designing the interface of a social machine, realize that people are likely to feel empathy and be willing to talk openly with the machine or robot. Think ahead about how you will handle issues of confidentiality and privacy.

☑ When you want people to feel empathy, make the machine a little bit like a human.

☑ Don't ask people to do things to machines or robots that they would be uncomfortable doing to another person (for example, acting threatening or violent).

HOW CREATIVITY INFLUENCES DESIGN

Most of this book is about the people you're designing for. But this chapter is especially for *you*, the designer. It explains the latest research on creativity and the brain, so you can apply that research to your work and use it to improve your creativity and product design.

47 EVERYONE CAN BE CREATIVE

Creativity isn't a trait that some people have and others don't. Before I explain why that's true, let me first define what I mean by creativity. If 100 people looked at the same abstract painting by Jackson Pollock, many of them might say, "Oh, that artist is really creative," but not everyone. If 100 people watched the TV series *So You Think You Can Dance,* many of them might say, "The dancers are creative," or "The choreographers are creative." If 100 people listened to music by Philip Glass, some might say, "That composer is creative."

What if 100 people went to a fashion show? Would everyone say that the clothing designers are creative? Or what if they saw a graffiti artist's work on a wall—would they say that the artist is creative? What about people who design technology? Are they creative?

There are many possible definitions of creativity. We probably won't agree entirely on the definition or on the results. However, here's a definition I've put together that I find descriptive and useful:

Creativity is the **process** of generating new ideas, possibilities, or alternatives that result in **outcomes** that are **original** and of **value**.

Here's why I like this definition:

- **Process**—The word "process" is in the definition. So, creativity isn't a trait that some people have and other people don't. There's actually a creative process that you can follow.

- **Outcomes**—Just doing the process isn't necessarily being creative. If you follow a creative process, and by doing so you end up with something, that's an outcome. Being creative means that you have something when you're done.

- **Original**—The definition includes the word "original." Being creative isn't just copying what somebody else did. When you're creative, you end up with something unique.

- **Value**—When you're creative, the outcome is of value to someone. It doesn't have to be of value to everyone, but it has to be of value to someone.

Even with this definition, we may not necessarily agree on who's creative and who's not. But the definition gives us a place to start talking about creativity, and a way to evaluate whether or not a particular activity is creative.

MYTHS ABOUT CREATIVITY

Let's clear up some myths about creativity:

1. Some people are "naturally" creative and other people aren't.

    It's true that some people spend more time in creative activity than others. But brain science is clear about the fact that there are creative brain states that can be turned on by some fairly simple actions. This means that everyone can learn how to be more creative.

2. Creativity means creating "works of art."

    Being creativity doesn't equate only with creating fine art, such as painting a landscape or writing a symphony. There are many ways to be creative, and creating works of art is just one way. Creativity includes many things, for example, cooking, programming, interface design, and problem solving.

3. Some people are left-brained (analytical) and others are right-brained (creative).

    My PhD research was on the right and left halves of the brain, so I can get pretty involved in a conversation about the subject. The human brain has two hemispheres: the left and the right. It's a common misconception that the left side of the brain is all about being logical and analytical and rational, and the right side of the brain is all about being intuitive and creative. That description is not accurate.

Here's a summary of what's true and what's myth:

● There are definitely two sides to the brain—the left and the right—and it's true that there are some brain structures on one side that aren't on the other. For instance, the ability to speak and to understand language is on the left, and some spatial awareness is on the right. However, it's simplistic to say that when you listen to music, you're listening to it only with the right side of your brain. Even people who don't play an instrument show activity on both sides of the brain when listening to music. (Although those who play an instrument show more activity in more areas of the brain than those who don't.) It's simplistic to say that the right side is the creative side.

● The corpus callosum is a bundle of nerve fibers that connects the left and right halves of the brain. Information (nerve impulses) passes through the corpus callosum very quickly. So even if something started on one side of the brain, it doesn't stay there very long.

- When people say "I'm a left-brained person" or "I'm a right-brained person," they're actually not referring to sides of the brain. They're referring to styles of thinking, learning, or processing information. There are different ways to process information, but they don't correspond to specific halves of the brain.

Hopefully this debunks some of the myths. So if these aren't true, what *is* true about brain science and creativity?

The rest of this chapter describes the research on the brain and creativity as well as the implications for what you can do to stimulate creativity in yourself and others.

Takeaways

☑ Don't worry about being right-brained or left-brained. Everyone can apply what they know about brain science to be more creative.

☑ You don't have to be "artistic" to be creative. You can be creative no matter what you're doing. For example, you can creatively solve a problem.

---

48 CREATIVITY STARTS WITH THE EXECUTIVE ATTENTION NETWORK

You may associate creativity with being loose and free. You may imagine a painter having no plan and throwing paint at a canvas to see what happens. You may imagine a composer sitting at a piano and letting his hands wander up and down the keys to just hear what sounds might come out. Exploring your tools or instruments now and then in an unconstrained way is probably a good idea, and may at some point help you to be more creative, but this isn't the process that leads to creativity most of the time.

Research on the brain and creativity tells us that the first step in creativity is to focus intensely. Whether you're trying to solve a problem at work or create a new musical masterpiece, being creative starts with focus.

BRAIN NETWORKS, NOT STRUCTURES

When most writers write about the brain (including me), they tend to write about particular brain areas, for example, the fusiform facial area for processing human faces, or the parts of the brain that process sound, or emotions. Vinod Menon and Steven Bressler (2010) started writing a few years ago about what they call "large-scale brain networks."

Instead of thinking about particular structures in the brain, neuroscientists, following Menon and Bressler's lead, are now looking at how different parts of the brain are networked together, what each particular network does, and even how the networks interact. These brain networks are a critical part of understanding the neuroscience of creativity.

THE EXECUTIVE ATTENTION NETWORK

The first network you need to know about is the executive attention network. When this network is active, you're concentrating. And it turns out that if you want to be creative, then the first thing you need to do is activate the executive attention network. Creativity starts with intense focus on an issue, an idea, or a problem. This is when you set your intention for the problem to be solved, or the creative idea to be worked on.

Note The executive attention network includes part of the outer area of the prefrontal cortex and some areas at the back of the parietal lobe.

ASK THE RIGHT QUESTION

To use your executive attention network to help you creatively solve a problem or come up with a new idea, make sure you're focusing on the right problem or idea.

You can get so caught up in the problem you're trying to solve, or the creative idea you want to come up with, that you focus immediately on the solution. But before you focus on the solution, you have to ask the right question. If you don't start with the right question, then your executive attention network will be focusing on the wrong issue.

Here's an example from one of my clients, an online clothing retailer. "We have these videos that show some of our most popular apparel items," the client told me. "How can we get people to watch more videos at our website? If people watch the videos, they're more likely to buy the product, and so we want to know how we can change the product page so that the videos display right away and automatically."

That's an example of *not* asking the right question. If we didn't stop and ask, "Is that the right question?" we might have come up with a creative solution like having the videos start as soon as the customer gets to the product page. But is that the best, most creative solution?

There are several other questions that might be better to concentrate on, for example:

"Why aren't people watching the videos?"

or

"Are there other design changes we could make that would increase sales?"

When you're trying to solve a problem or come up with a new idea, make sure you're asking the right question. Don't assume that the question at hand is the best or right one. Give the executive attention network the best question to concentrate on.

Takeaways

☑ To spark your creativity, ask yourself a question or set your intention. This will activate your executive attention network. Be specific about what you're going to work on.

☑ Make sure you're asking the right question. Spend time crafting the question so your brain networks will be solving the best problem or giving you ideas for the best outcome.

49 TO BE CREATIVE, ENGAGE THE BRAIN'S DEFAULT NETWORK

You're at work, it's after lunch, and you realize you're sitting at your desk, staring into space, and not thinking about anything in particular. Your brain is, relatively speaking, at rest. Your mind is wandering. What would your brain activity show at this moment?

The default network engages when you're not doing anything in particular. You could say that it's your brain activity when your brain is at rest, but the truth is that there's a lot of brain activity when the default network is operating.

Randy Buckner, a neuroscientist at Harvard, first wrote about the default network in a 2008 journal article. The default network was discovered accidentally. Researchers were studying the brain activity of people who were given certain tasks to do. Some participants in the study were told just to sit and think about nothing in particular as part of a control condition in the experiments. Initially this data was not even analyzed, but some researchers began to notice that there was quite a lot of brain activity in certain areas when people were supposedly not thinking about anything in particular.

THE BRAIN ISN'T REALLY AT REST

Even though the default network was initially considered brain activity during a resting state, the brain is actually just as active—or more active—in this state than when it's working on a specific task. Researchers now think of this not as a resting state, but as more of an internally focused state.

Continued research on the default network shows that it's active when people are exploring mental simulations—when they're preparing for events that they think may happen, before they happen. When people run through simulations based on their past experiences, when they think about the future, when they imagine alternative scenarios, and when they think about the perspectives of others in their situation—it's this default network that is active.

Note The default network includes inner parts of the prefrontal cortex and temporal lobe, as well as some regions of the parietal cortex.

THE DEFAULT NETWORK'S ROLE IN CREATIVITY

As noted earlier in this chapter, the creative process starts when you focus on an idea or a problem with the executive attention network. The default network is involved in the next step in the creative process. The default network runs through alternatives for the idea or problem you're trying to solve.

The default network does simulations, goes through your memory to look for things that you've experienced in the past that might be relevant, and imagines possible alternatives ideas and solutions.

The default network is critical for the creative process. It's important to set the idea or problem in the executive attention network first, but then you have to stop using the executive attention network. The two networks can't operate at the same time. You need the default network to look for ideas and connections, and run through possible alternatives. If you keep concentrating on the problem or idea, then you're using the executive attention network and not your default network. You have to step away if you want to be creative.

Why stepping away makes you more creative

How do you stop the executive attention network from working? Go do something else. Take a break, especially one that doesn't involve concentrated thinking. Go for a walk, weed the garden, take a shower, or clean up the house, and then your default network can activate.

 Take breaks while writing

I get a lot of exercise and a clean house when I'm writing a book. I'll start working on a new chapter and then have to go do something else. I take a walk, do some yoga, wash the dishes, or do laundry. This book is no exception!

Takeaways

☑ Once you set the intention or ask the right question of the executive attention network, the next step in the creative process is to *stop* thinking about the problem or idea so the default network can engage.

☑ When you have a problem to solve or need a creative idea, take a break and do something that requires little or no concentrated thought.

50 INDUCE AN "AHA" MOMENT

We've all had the experience: you're trying to solve a problem or come up with a new idea. You've been sitting at your desk, or discussing it in meetings, but you haven't come up with a solution or the right idea. Then you step away—go for a walk, go to lunch, do some housework, or go to sleep (engage the default network)—and suddenly you have an "aha" moment. The answer comes to you in a flash. Why does that happen?

So far this chapter has discussed the first two steps in the creative process:

1. Setting the problem or idea with the executive attention network.

2. Stepping away to engage the default network.

The "aha" solution comes from the third network involved in the creative process: the salience network.

THE MONITOR

The salience network constantly monitors everything that's going on in your brain. It monitors the stream of information coming in externally from the senses, and it monitors the executive attention network and the default network. The salience network monitors it all. It compares all the possible alternatives that the default network came up with against the problem or idea set in the executive attention network. When it finds the best (most salient) alternative, the salience network brings that idea to consciousness, and you have the "aha" moment.

The salience network works best if you've asked a clear question or posed a clear problem or idea in the executive attention network, and if you've stepped away and stopped using your prefrontal cortex so that the default network has been engaged.

THREE NETWORKS WORKING TOGETHER

People who are productively creative follow a process that includes these three networks. Your creative process may be specific to you, but to maximize your creativity, be sure you're using the three networks. Here's an example of the process:

1. Write down your initial ideas in a notebook or draw a picture of the problem you want to solve to ensure that you are spending some concentrated time focusing on the problem. This is the executive attention network.

2. Step away, whether it's to take a walk, listen to music, or clean the house. It doesn't matter how you do it as long as you step away. This is the default network.

3. Be prepared to grab the "aha" ideas when they come. Because the salience network does its work behind the scenes, you don't have to do anything in particular to get it to work.

Takeaways

☑ Your creative process should include time to concentrate on the idea or problem.

☑ Your creative process should include time to step away.

☑ Always carry a recording device or pen and paper with you, because you never know when the salience network will do its work and provide you with an answer.

☑ When you're problem solving or working creatively with a team, follow the same rhythm.

51 DAYDREAMING ENCOURAGES CREATIVITY

Now that you know about the three brain networks that are involved in the creative process, there's some related research to be aware of.

Some of this research focused on daydreaming. Daydreaming refers to the thoughts and images people have when their attention turns inward—when they're in default network mode.

Most scientists today use the term "mind wandering" instead of daydreaming. This is probably because the term "daydreaming" has taken on negative connotations.

Rebecca McMillan (2013) wrote about the history of research into daydreaming. The first scientist to study daydreaming was Jerome Singer, starting in 1955.

PRODUCTIVE VS. PATHOLOGICAL

Most psychologists in Singer's early research years thought daydreaming was nonproductive and even pathological. Singer was the first researcher to claim that positive constructive daydreaming was normal, widespread, and happens up to 50 percent of the time for most people. And he was the first researcher to make the connection between daydreaming and creativity.

Singer actually divided daydreaming into three types: positive constructive daydreaming (wishful thinking, creative thoughts), guilty-dysphoric daydreaming (obsessive thoughts and fantasies), and poor attentional control (an inability to concentrate on the task at hand). Only positive constructive daydreaming is related to the default network.

Note Daydreaming can be intentional or it can happen without you realizing you've slipped into it. You can, however, tell when people are daydreaming: their pupils dilate and they blink more (Romain Grandchamp, 2011).

GETTING OVER THE BAD RAP OF DAYDREAMING

Despite the research about the importance of daydreaming to creativity, many people are still uncomfortable with the idea. Many of us grew up getting into trouble for daydreaming, because the adults in our lives took it to mean that we were goofing off, or not paying attention.

And as adults, many of us work in corporate cultures that also say it's not OK for us to sit at our desks, stare off into space, and "do nothing" for a while. It might actually be the most productive thing you can do.

Takeaways

☑ Don't be afraid to daydream. It will heighten your creativity.

☑ When you work in a place that discourages daydreaming, share the research on daydreaming with the people you work with and with your supervisor.

☑ When you're working on a creative idea or solving a problem, set aside specific time for daydreaming every day until the solution or idea comes to you.

52 SLEEPING ENCOURAGES CREATIVITY

You've learned about the positive effect that daydreaming has on creativity. The same is true for sleep, but it works on the brain in a different way than daydreaming.

BOOST YOUR CREATIVITY BY AT LEAST 33 PERCENT

If I told you that there's a way to boost your creativity by at least 33 percent and that this method is free, you might be skeptical. But as you've probably already guessed, the answer is sleep!

The 33 percent figure comes from Jeffrey Ellenbogen, the director of the Sleeping Brain Lab at Massachusetts General Hospital.

Psychologists and neuroscientists have been trying to figure out what sleep is all about for decades.

LISTENING TO BRAIN WAVES IN SLEEPING RATS

A breakthrough in understanding sleep and learning came from Matthew Wilson because of a small mistake he made in the lab.

Wilson (now at MIT) was working with rats in lab experiments on learning. He recorded signals from the rats' brains while they were running mazes in the lab. One day he accidentally left the equipment hooked up. The rats were sleeping, but the equipment was still recording their brain signals.

When he compared the signals from the sleeping rats, he found that the signals matched the brain activity when the rats were awake and running the maze. The rats were re-running the maze in their sleep.

CONSOLIDATING INFORMATION DURING SLEEP

Since then, sleep researchers have delved more into sleep. They now know that when people sleep, they review things they learned while awake that day. They "decide" (even though they're asleep and unaware of deciding) what to keep and what to let go of from what they learned during the day.

There are four stages of sleep. A series of research studies at Robert Stickgold's Sleep Research Lab at the Harvard Medical School shows that people jettison most of their memories of what happened during the day in Stages 1 and 2, and they transfer the memories they want to keep to long-term memory during REM sleep. REM sleep is also when most people dream.

A small group of cells in the brain stem affect proteins in the amygdala and hippo-campus in the brain. These cells are responsible for memory consolidation during sleep.

THE CONNECTION BETWEEN SLEEP AND CREATIVITY

This reviewing and consolidation of information during sleep has an effect on creativity. A large part of being creative is making connections between new information and existing information in memory. This is part of what's happening during consolidation when people sleep. The time connection between concentrated executive attention network focus (discussed earlier in this chapter) and sleep is important, too. For optimal creative output, you need to set that intention not too long before going to sleep.

Note In terms of creativity, naps can also improve your creativity, but only if you're able to go into REM sleep.

Takeaways

☑ Restate or write down the problem you're trying solve or the creative idea you're seeking progress on an hour or two before you go to bed.

☑ Get a good night's rest (at least six hours—eight would be better). Naps might help, but only if you enter REM sleep.

☑ Keep a pen and paper or recorder handy. Often the answers and ideas you're looking for will come right upon awakening.

53 NOISE AND MUSIC INCREASE CREATIVITY

As I'm writing this chapter, I'm sitting in a Starbucks. A lot of my work involves activities for which I need a very quiet environment, but when I'm writing, I'm more creative and more productive when I have some amount of visual and auditory stimulation. So I head to a coffee shop. I call it the "coffee shop effect."

Although I haven't yet found the research that would support the idea that stimulation of peripheral vision increases creativity (I'm still looking), there *is* research that shows that noise and music increase creativity.

QUIET ISN'T NECESSARILY A GOOD THING

When it comes to creativity, being in a very quiet environment isn't always a good thing. Ravi Mehta (2012) tested how much noise was ideal for increasing creativity. 50 dB (decibels) was not enough noise, and 85 dB was too much. The best level seems to be around 70 dB, which is about the level at a coffee shop, taking into account the general noise level from the espresso machine, conversations, and perhaps music. Mehta concluded that as noise levels increased, so did abstract thinking. When the noise reaches too high a level, abstract thinking continues, but there's too much distraction for creative thinking—hence the "just right" middle amount of noise.

DEBUNKING THE MOZART EFFECT

You may have heard about the Mozart effect. This popular theory from the 1990s stated that listening to Mozart would make people perform better on tests, make them smarter, and make them more creative. It has since been debunked. But not the entire theory has been debunked.

It turns out there *is* a Mozart effect—and a Bach effect, and a Taylor Swift effect. It's a "listen to music you like" effect. In fact, it's not really a music effect. Even listening to audio books can boost people's ability to solve visual problems after they listen (Naintais, 1999). In fact, listening to *anything* they like helps people solve problems better afterwards. The idea is that the audio puts people in a better mood, which makes them perform better.

But what about creativity—does listening to music make you creative *while* you're listening?

MUSIC AND THE DEFAULT NETWORK

Remember the discussion of the default network and creativity earlier in this chapter? According to Daniel Levitin, author of *The Organized Mind*, listening to music activates the default network, which as we saw before, increases creativity.

Takeaways

- ☑ To increase creativity, don't work in a totally silent environment. Have a moderate level of noise (70 dB).

- ☑ To increase creativity, listen to music you like. This will activate your default network.

---

54 PEOPLE ARE MORE CREATIVE WITHIN SOME CONSTRAINTS

Before you continue in this chapter, I'd like you to do a short exercise. **Do *not* read ahead.** Do Step 1 first before reading any further:

> **Step 1**: Get a pen or pencil and a piece of paper, and take up to 30 seconds to write down as many things that are white as you can think of. Not things that could be white (for example, a shirt could be white or blue or green), but things that are usually white. Begin!

Ok, now do the second part of the exercise:

> **Step 2:** Get your pen and paper ready again, and this time take up to 30 seconds to write down things to either eat or drink that are white. Begin.

Count up how many items you have on each list.

I got this exercise from Keith Sawyer's book *Zig Zag: The Surprising Path To Greater Creativity.* The point of the exercise has to do with constraints. Most of the time when I have people do this exercise, they come up with more items in Step 2 than in Step 1. That's because the second time the instructions included constraints.

SOME CONSTRAINTS ENHANCE CREATIVITY

We usually think that to be creative, it's best to have as few constraints as possible—maximum freedom. I've heard designers say, "You've imposed too many constraints for me to come up with a creative solution." When I've had a client that wants the design team to follow an existing style guide, or use an existing pattern library, some members of the team will complain, "All these constraints limit our creativity."

It's certainly true that too many constraints can and often do limit creativity, but having no or too few constraints also hampers creativity.

If you have no or few constraints, then you also have a less-defined problem or design space. It will be harder to set a specific intention about what you're designing or solving. This means that the executive attention network discussed earlier in the chapter won't have a clear idea of what to focus on. And the first step in being more creative is to stimulate that executive attention network with a clear intention.

What constraints you should impose, and how many, depend on what you're designing. Here are some examples of constraints you could put on a design or a project:

- Limit colors
- Limit size
- Limit shape
- Use a particular style guide
- Use a particular set of design patterns
- Do the work in a limited time frame

Takeaways

☑ Try applying some constraints on your next design.

☑ When you're working with a team, get the team to agree on some constraints, at least initially. Have them do the constraints exercise at the beginning of this section if they need convincing.

55 THE RIGHT KIND OF COLLABORATION INCREASES CREATIVITY

I tend toward introversion. When I tell people that, they usually don't believe me. I like being on stage: giving talks at conferences, performing in local community theater productions, singing as a jazz vocalist with a small ensemble. So when I tell people I'm an introvert, they usually laugh. "I am!" I assure them.

As an introvert, I like working alone. But I also know that I'm more creative when I'm collaborating with others, and not just collaborating asynchronously through email or sharing documents, but collaborating with others in real time.

I'm probably not alone, however, in my reaction to the suggestion that we all get together and brainstorm. I have to admit that sometimes I cringe. It's partially because I'm an introvert. But it's also because brainstorming can be ineffective and even harmful to creative collaboration if done incorrectly. There's a right way and a wrong way to do brainstorming.

DOING BRAINSTORMING THE RIGHT WAY

In case you've somehow managed to avoid participating in a brainstorming session, here's how brainstorming often works: A group of people convene in a room together with an idea or a problem to solve. Everyone comes up with ideas, and the usual rule is that ideas are not judged or criticized until later—the goal is to generate as many ideas as possible as quickly as possible. One person is usually assigned to be the scribe, and this person writes down the ideas on a flipchart or whiteboard.

Scott Isaksen and John Gaulin (2005) reviewed dozens of research studies on brainstorming, and did some of their own research. Here's what they concluded:

- The instructions that people are given are important. In one study, when the researchers gave the group the instruction to generate five to seven ideas, the group produced seven ideas. When they gave the instruction to generate at least 20 ideas, the group produced 21 ideas. When the instructions did not include a number, the group generated 29 ideas.

- Having a trained facilitator to lead the group has a huge (positive) impact. The groups with a trained facilitator produced more ideas by a factor of 5 to 1 over groups without a trained facilitator.

- Some of the groups used a variation of brainstorming called "brainwriting." Brainwriting is different than brainstorming: people write down their own ideas first, then hand that paper to the person on the right, who adds more ideas and hands the paper to the right, and so on.

- The groups using brainwriting and a facilitator came up with more ideas and better ideas than any other groups. When the facilitator participated in coming up with ideas (not just leading the group), then the group effect was even stronger.

- Individuals working alone generated fewer ideas than any of the brainstorming or brainwriting groups. The differences were striking. The brainstorming groups with facilitators generated an average of 126.5 unique (nonredundant) ideas per group. People working on their own, not in a group, generated 58 unique ideas. The brainwriting groups, with facilitators, generated an average of 208 unique ideas.

BRAINWRITING AS AN ANTIDOTE TO ANCHORING

One of the reasons that brainwriting is better than brainstorming is that it avoids anchoring. In brainstorming, someone comes up with an idea first and says it out loud. As soon as that idea is mentioned, it can act as an anchor and may influence all the other ideas people come up with. With brainwriting, no one "goes first," so there's no anchoring, and as a result there are usually more diverse ideas.

Another reason brainwriting works better than brainstorming is that quiet people, who may not shout out ideas in a regular brainstorming session, have the chance to have as much input as everyone else.

Note Loran Nordgren, a professor at the Kellogg School of Management, created an app for brainstorming called Candor. The app has people come up with ideas before joining the group. Then the group goes through and evaluates the ideas.

Takeaways

- ☑ Collaborating with brainstorming can be a good way to generate ideas, but use the variant of brainwriting instead of brainstorming to come up with more diverse ideas.

- ☑ Use a trained facilitator for brainstorming/writing and let him or her participate in the generation of ideas.

56 BEING A PERFECTIONIST CAN RUIN CREATIVE WORK

It's my opinion (uncorroborated by any science that I know about) that people who are drawn to design tend to be perfectionists. Being a designer, and being creative, means that you have an idea in your head about how something should be, and you work on it as long and hard as you can to get it to match what's in you head. It's like the quote attributed to Michelangelo:

> I saw the angel in the marble and carved until I set him free.

You'd think that wanting perfection would be a good trait in a creative person, and often it is. But perfectionism can also be detrimental to creativity.

Brian Sullivan spoke at SXSW in 2015 about the downside of perfectionism. He talks about research by Brené Brown that connects perfectionism with shame. Perfectionists have a hard time taking criticism. They tend to equate criticism with proof that they're wrong. If perfectionists are afraid of being exposed as a fraud, then they'll fear change and collaboration.

FEAR OF FAILURE

We all have fear of failure sometimes, but perfectionists have this fear more than most. Failure, in many cultures, for example, in the United States, is seen as a bad thing—it's not good to fail. This is not true in all cultures. In some schools, in some cultures (for example, in some schools in France and in Asia), children learn that struggling and making mistakes are good. They're taught that the whole class can learn from the mistakes and failures of one student.

Changing the idea of failure from a bad thing into a process often enhances creativity. There's the famous quote attributed to Thomas Edison:

> I have not failed. I've just found 10,000 ways that won't work.

He purportedly said this when he was trying to find a good filament for the light bulb. And indeed, he had tried many different types of filaments, and ways to use them that had not worked. But he didn't consider these attempts to be failures. He just thought of them as part of an iterative process. By going through all the different possible filament materials, he believed he would eventually find the right one.

If you're open to the idea that failure is iterative, then you can accept that you may not get the most creative idea right away, that you're not going to solve the problem necessarily with the first idea you come up with, and that you don't have to come up with perfect, fully formed ideas. You can get past the idea of failure. If you're afraid of failing, then you're going to be afraid of starting. Assume that you won't have perfect ideas at the start, and see if you can get to the point where you think that's OK. Turning the idea of failure into an idea of iteration is a great way to generate creative solutions.

The same applies to designing with a team. The team needs to iterate to get to a good design, too.

Takeaways

☑ Be on the look out for perfectionists on your team—yourself included. You might need to get some coaching to relax and lose some fear.

☑ Make sure you and your team have time and cycles available to iterate. This lets you come up with ideas and try them out, discarding them till you get to the idea or solution that fits best.

HOW PEOPLE'S BODIES AFFECT DESIGN

If you design physical objects for people to use, then you probably think about how bodies influence design. But many designers primarily design for screens and displays. If that's you, then you may not think a lot about how bodies affect design beyond eyes (to see the displays) and fingers (typing and clicking).

You might be surprised to find out how significantly the human body affects design, for example:

- People don't actually think with just their brains. The latest research shows that moving the body changes thoughts and feelings.

- Design is moving beyond keyboards, mice, track pads, and a few gestures. With more complicated gestures and with augmented and virtual reality expanding, the human body is becoming a critical design factor.

57 PEOPLE THINK AND FEEL WITH THEIR BODIES

If you think about why people think, feel, and behave in certain ways, you probably think about what's going on in their brains. You might not realize how much people's bodies influence their behavior. The field of "embodied cognition" is gaining more ground in cognitive science, psychology, and design. It's the idea that people's bodies—their size, shape, and movement—not only contribute to how they think and their behavior, but also actually drive their thinking and their behavior.

CATCHING A FLY BALL

The classic example to explain embodied cognition is the example of how a baseball outfielder catches a fly ball. Let's say you're the outfielder and a fly ball is coming toward you. It's your job to catch it. How do you get to the right location at the right moment to catch the ball?

It's a difficult task. You're very far away from the batter and the ball will appear very small until it gets close to you. It's all going to happen very quickly. You have to move from wherever you are on the field to the exact location where the ball will land at some point in the future. You don't know exactly when that will be, or exactly where it will be.

A regular cognitive science brain model to explain how you catch the ball goes like this:

You have a mental representation of the motion of the ball, information about the speed with which it might be traveling, and information about direction. You predict the future location and timing of the ball using physics. Since the ball is being thrown near the Earth's surface, it moves in a curved path. The only force acting on it is gravity. If you know the size, mass, direction, speed, and angle, then you can use this information to predict the location of the ball. Your brain does these calculations and then gives commands to your motor system to move you to the right location in time.

Interestingly, if this were really what you would do, you'd move in a straight line right to the location. How many times have you seen outfielders move in a perfectly straight line from where they are to where the ball is going to be? They usually start in one direction, but then pause or speed up. They move backward, forward, or sideways. They rarely, if ever, move in a straight line right to the ball.

The embodied cognition explanation is different. The brain doesn't have to calculate anything. According to the embodied cognition viewpoint, if you were really mentally computing physics calculations, you'd make too many errors. The ball is so far away that you could barely perceive it. You wouldn't be able to get the data you need to make the calculations.

The embodied cognition viewpoint says that you would use "kinematic" information—information about how things are changing over time in relation to your body. The physics of the ball make it at first rise and then gravity makes it slow down. It reaches a peak height and then accelerates as it starts to fall on the other side of the arc. You see this motion and use the "kinematic" information it communicates.

It turns out there are two strategies you can use within the embodied cognition explanation:

1. If you're in a direct line with the arc of the ball, then you can use your eyes and your muscles to move you. If the ball appears to move at a constant velocity (speed and direction), and if you keep adjusting your location and movement so that it still appears to move at a constant velocity, then you'll end up in the right place at the right time.

2. If you're not in a direct line with the arc of the fly ball, then you use your eyes and your muscles to move in a way that makes the ball look linear. The trajectory of the ball is actually curved, but as long as you keep moving in a way that the ball looks like it's moving linearly, then you'll be at the location where the ball is when it arrives.

Experiments designed to see if people actually move in these paths when catching a ball show that they do (and so do dogs when they're catching objects thrown at them).

THE PROOF IS WITH THE ROBOTS

If the baseball thought experiment didn't convince you about embodied cognition, then perhaps these robot comparisons will.

The ASIMO robot was built from a traditional cognitive science approach. It has programs that control its movement. It can walk and (sometimes) climb stairs. But any disruption that doesn't fit this programming causes disaster (http://www.youtube.com/watch?v=ASoCJTYgYB0). It does fine until something unexpected happens—something it hasn't been programmed for.

Compare ASIMO to Boston Dynamics' BigDog (http://www.youtube.com/watch?v=cNZPRsrwumQ). BigDog is built from the embodied cognition viewpoint. BigDog was built to walk on uneven ground. Instead of complicated software to control movements, BigDog responds to what happens in its environment through feedback from its "legs."

The more designers understand how people move and interact with the world, and then apply that knowledge to the design of machines, the more the machines come to resemble people in terms of how they interact with the world.

Designers have a tendency to focus on the visual aspects of design. It's true that vision is a critical sense, but what happens if you start to include the implications of the body for design? People are moving all the time, and their movement is part of their decision-making. If you design a product that's visually appealing and fits the context only visually, you could end up designing a product that's unappealing or unusable.

 People are more satisfied with a choice when they engage in a physical act of closure

Imagine that you're sitting in a tea shop looking at the menu, deciding what tea you want to order. You make your choice and close the menu.

What you may not realize is that because you closed the menu after making your choice, you'll be more satisfied with the choice than if you hadn't closed the menu. It's a version of embodied cognition: the physical act of closure changes your emotional response.

This tea experiment was actually conducted by Yangjie Gu (2013). Gu told the participants in the experiment that once they decided, they could not change their minds. Participants who were told to close the menu were more satisfied with the tea they chose than those who didn't close the menu.

Takeaways

☑ When you design products and product interfaces, keep in mind the body and muscle movement required and the context in which the product will be used.

☑ When you do user research, include research on how people are moving when they use your product.

☑ When you storyboard and sketch your design, include information in the storyboard on how people are moving while they use your product.

58 PEOPLE NATURALLY GESTURE

Tell a friend about the last time you went to visit a family member, and you'll notice that you're moving your hands and arms while telling the story. Your body is gesturing without you even thinking about it.

GESTURING TO MANIPULATE A DEVICE

As designers, we're now building in gestures as a way for users to interact with and manipulate interfaces. We've been designing interactions with keyboards, mice, trackballs, track pads, pens, and touching with fingers. And now we're using more complicated hand, finger, and body movements as gestures for interacting with device interfaces. Just listing some of the finger and hand controls on a smartphone shows the variation:

- Touch
- Touch and drag
- Tap once with one finger
- Tap twice with one finger
- Tap once with two fingers
- Swipe with one finger

- Swipe with two fingers
- Swipe with three fingers
- Flick
- Pinch closed with two fingers
- Spread open with two fingers
- Rotate

And so on.

The ability of devices to understand gestures is increasing. The latest technologies use radar to detect and interpret human gestures and then connect them to a device so that people can control the device by making gestures near it. It's now possible for people to "grab" something on a screen by making a grabbing motion in the air, or hold out a hand with the palm facing out to tell a robot to stop.

 Why people gesture

It's often thought that people gesture while they talk to convey information. Although that's true, the latest theory is that the most important reason people gesture is because they need to gesture in order to think. It's another example of embodied cognition.

NATURAL GESTURES VERSUS FORCED GESTURES

While many gestures come naturally, others don't. Moving a finger clockwise to signify that you want to rotate something is a natural gesture, as is holding up your hand with your palm out to tell someone or something to stop. Swiping with two fingers to mean one thing and swiping with three fingers to mean something else are not natural gestures.

Should people have to learn new gestures that aren't natural to them in order to interact with devices? I don't have a definitive answer to this question yet. On the one hand (embodied cognition metaphor!), people often learn new movements to interact with devices. Many people type quickly on a keyboard without thinking about it, yet this is something they had to learn. But if they have to read a manual to find out what gestures to use in order to use a device, maybe those gestures aren't the best way to interact with the device. Did the designer invest enough design time, energy, and knowledge in the interaction decisions when designing this device? Or, rather than taking the time up front to design the interface so that a limited set of natural gestures would encompass all the needed tasks, did the designer optimize the technology and just throw the human gestures needed to use it on top?

Takeaways

- ☑ People like using natural gestures rather than always having to type or touch.

- ☑ When you're choosing gestures for people to use when interacting with a product, choose gestures that come naturally whenever possible.

- ☑ When you're designing a product that will respond to human gestures, allow enough time in the project planning to decide on and test the gestures.

59 PEOPLE HAVE PHYSICAL LIMITATIONS OF MOVEMENT

If you ask someone to turn a button or knob that's 8 inches (20 cm) in diameter, that's going to be difficult, or even impossible, to do with one hand. People have physical limitations of movement, and range of motion based on body size and physical structure. If you're an industrial designer, then you're probably familiar with human factors and ergonomic standards.

But if you don't have experience designing products that require body movement, you may need to learn about human factors and ergonomic standards in order to design for gestures, and augmented and virtual realities.

Note If you need a reference book on human physical averages and limitations, check out Human Factors Design Handbook (1992) by Wesley Woodson, Peggy Tillman, and Barry Tillman. A new edition, titled Human Factors and Ergonomics Design Handbook, is due out in February 2016.

AUGMENTED AND VIRTUAL REALITY

Imagine that you're sitting in your office. There's a desk and the chair you're sitting in. But you're in an augmented office, so in addition to you being able to see the actual office and furniture, you can see objects that are not physically present, but are being superimposed on your vision. For example, on your desk you may "see" files and documents. To your right, you might "see" a filing cabinet. In this space, you can move your body and interact with the real, physical objects as well as the added objects that aren't actually there. This is augmented reality. Sometimes the term "mediated reality" is used instead of augmented reality. Augmented reality implies that there is "more." Mediated reality doesn't imply more—it implies that the reality is altered, but it may be more, less, or the same in terms of quantity.

Augmented and mediated reality environments open up a world of possibilities in terms of interacting with both real and simulated objects using gestures.

Virtual reality is more limiting than augmented or mediated reality environments. Rather than interacting with both real and simulated environments at the same time, virtual reality constructs an environment that is not real at all, but entirely simulated. Although you can use gestures and turn your head, you can't move around freely in virtual reality the way you can in augmented reality (or you're likely to bump into actual objects that aren't part of the world you're viewing).

Note One reason augmented and virtual reality is powerful and holds promise for rich interactions is because people react to simulated environments as though they were real. Even if people know they're interacting in a simulated or virtual environment, they react and behave as though the environment is real.

Takeaways

- ☑ If you're not familiar with human factor ergonomic standards, familiarize yourself with them so you're ready to design interfaces with gestures.

- ☑ If you haven't personally experienced augmented or virtual reality devices, try them out so you'll have a mental model of what the experience is like before you're asked to participate in the design of one.

60 THUMBS CAN REACH ONLY SO FAR

As I'm writing this book, the size of smartphone screens ranges from 3.5 inches to 6 inches. Our design and implementation tools let us design the screens without having to know or design for the exact size. If the software, site, or app is designed well, what appears on the screen at any given time varies automatically according to the size of the screen.

What doesn't vary automatically is the human hand and the human thumb. If you want to design a screen that's easy and efficient to use, then you have to design for how people use their hands, fingers, and thumbs on a small to mid-size screen.

THE MYTH OF ONE-HANDED USE

Conventional wisdom holds that people mainly use their smartphones with one hand—that they hold the phone in their dominant hand and use the dominant thumb to tap and navigate. This does happen some of the time, but people also use the non-dominant hand some of the time, and sometimes they hold the phone in one hand and use the other hand for tapping.

THERE IS NO "OW" ZONE

You may have seen diagrams of a smartphone screen showing parts that are "natural" for the thumb to reach, parts that are a "stretch" for the thumb to reach, and parts that are marked "ow" for the thumb to reach. These are misleading since the thumb can't stretch that far. It's not that it hurts to reach further; it just doesn't reach. When people can't reach with their thumbs, they shift the position of the phone or use two hands.

Steven Hoober (2014) tested where 1,333 people tapped on a 5.1-inch screen smartphone. He found that:

- The center of the screen was the easiest to tap.

- The center of the screen was the most accurate and fastest target.

- People often shifted the way they were holding the phone to touch everywhere else on the screen.

- Most taps outside the central area involved two hands.

- People held their phones with one hand when they were looking at the phone or carrying it around, but they sometimes switched to two-handed use when they were actively interacting.

- People held the phone and used the thumb of that same hand for interactions 49 percent of the time.

- People frequently cradled the phone with one hand and used their index finger of the other.

To complicate matters further, the size and reach of people's thumbs vary widely.

THE "TOP-LEFT" STANDARD MUST GO

Since people are using their thumbs a lot and since the thumb doesn't easily reach the top left of the smartphone screen, it makes sense to *not* use the top left as a place for any important controls. Although using the top left, especially to display the "menu" icon, seems to be a standard at the moment, it's one of the worst places to put a frequently used control and will, most of the time, require a two-hand shift (Figure 60.1). It's better to put important controls in the center or on the bottom of the screen (Figure 60.2).

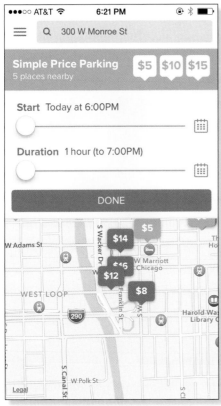

FIGURE 60.1 The top left is the standard, but it's a poor place for an important control, such as the menu icon.

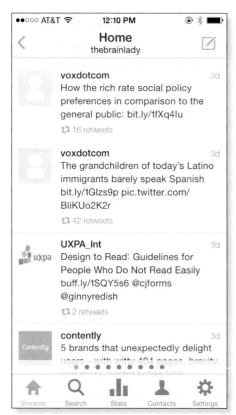

FIGURE 60.2 The center or bottom is better for important controls.

61 DISTANCE FROM THE SCREEN IS CRITICAL

Some designers have always designed for situations where people are at varying distances from the display, for example, signage in public places like train stations or airports, or displays on a factory floor or a hospital operating theatre.

But many designers are used to designing for people who are sitting in front of a desktop or a laptop. If that's true for you, then it may be new for you to think about the user's distance from the thing you're designing, and how that should affect your design.

IT'S DISTANCE, NOT RESOLUTION

Most designers are used to thinking about designing for different size screens (large monitor, regular desktop monitor, laptop, tablet, smartphone). And many designers are used to thinking about different screen resolutions. A 50-inch HDTV has a resolution of 1920 x 1080. But now many smartphones are also 1920 x 1080. Luke Wroblewski, a product director at Google, says that instead of designing for the screen resolution, you need to design for the distance that the viewer is from the screen.

In a talk Wroblewski gave in 2015 (www.lukew.com), he uses the example of someone viewing Netflix to choose a movie to watch. Here are typical viewing distances (Wroblewski gave them in feet, but I've added in metric measurements):

- Smartphone: 1 ft (~30.5 cm)
- Tablet: 1.5 ft (~46 cm)
- Laptop: 2 ft (~61 cm)
- TV: 10 ft (~ 3 meters)

Why does viewing distance matter? If people are at different viewing distances from the display, then the size of the objects on the display needs to change. When the icon is on a TV that's 10 feet away, the size of the movie icon needs to be 5.25 inches, or 13.33 cm high.

Figures 61.1, 61.2, 61.3, and 61.4 show the different sizes that the movie icons need to be on the display for the viewer to effectively browse the movie choices.

FIGURE 61.1 An icon on a smartphone needs to be 1 inch (~2.5 cm).

FIGURE 61.2 An icon on a tablet needs to be 1.75 inches (~4.5 cm).

FIGURE 61.3 An icon on a laptop needs to be 2.25 inches (~5.7 cm).

FIGURE 61.4 An icon on a TV needs to be 5.25 inches (~13.33 cm).

Takeaways

☑ Decide how large items need to be on the screen based on the viewer's distance from the screen.

☑ Use this rule of thumb when determining the size of images or targets on a display: for every foot (30 cm) you add in distance from the display, add 1/2 inch (1.3 cm) in size for the item on the display.

HOW PEOPLE SHOP AND BUY

Contrary to what you may hear, brick-and-mortar stores are not disappearing. According to the US Census Bureau, as of June 30, 2015, 92.8 percent of all retail sales in the US occur in a store and 7.2 percent are online. The percent of online sales is rising, however.

This means that digital designers in retail can't stop designing websites and apps for shoppers. Even though the vast majority of sales are occurring in stores, an increasing number of those in-store sales are "digical" sales: that is, they combine the digital and the physical.

62 PEOPLE DON'T SEPARATE SHOPPING ONLINE FROM SHOPPING IN A STORE

If you talk to major retailers in the US, it quickly becomes clear that online sales and store sales are two very different things. Several of my retail clients have online shopping operations and staff headquarters in one location, and store operations and staff in a different location, often thousands of miles away. From the retailer's point of view, there are two very different ways to buy stuff from them.

But people don't make those same distinctions. They buy from a brand. The big decision for the consumer is not whether to buy online at the Apple website or to make a trip to the nearest Apple store, but whether to buy an iPhone from Apple or whether to buy one from AT&T.

In fact, the act of shopping in a store now regularly includes shopping on a smartphone while shopping in the store. Here's a common scenario:

A shopper goes to the XYZ store and finds a shirt that she likes. But the store doesn't have the shirt in her size or in the color she wants. So, while she's in the store, she uses her smartphone to order the shirt from the XYZ website, which ships it directly to her home.

Is that sale counted as an online sale or an in-store sale? It's not necessarily one or the other.

GOING OMNICHANNEL

Retailers are learning that to succeed in retail today, they need to be true omnichannel retailers—meaning they need to provide a consistent experience across all online and store shopping channels.

Consider the following data about people and shopping from Darrell Rigby (2014) and the A. T. Kearney Omnichannel Consumer Preferences study (2014) (all data is from the US):

- People think shopping is fun and entertaining. They often want to go to a physical store with other people for a social experience.

- 90 percent of shoppers of all ages prefer to buy in a brick-and-mortar store.

- Even if people make their purchase online, they have often visited a store to do research before they buy.

- About half of all online sales are purchased from retailers that also have physical stores.

- People will often research a product online and then purchase it in a store. Their research includes looking at products at different websites, reading reviews, and comparing prices. This researching online and then purchasing in a store is called "webrooming."

- People will sometimes go to a store and then, while in the store, use their smartphone to look for a better price for the product they pick out. They may then order that product online. This going first to a store and then checking out prices in other places is called "showrooming."

Takeaways

☑ Break yourself of thinking of online shopping versus store shopping. Think omnichannel instead.

☑ Make it easy for people to shop your entire brand, whether in a store or online.

☑ Conduct research with your target audience to discover what makes shopping fun for the products you sell.

☑ Conduct research with your target audience to discover what the entire shopping process looks like for your customers. Evaluate whether you have a seamless online/store experience.

63 PEOPLE SPEND LESS WHEN THEY USE CASH

Budget and financial counselors often advise people to withdraw cash each week and use it to pay for daily and weekly expenses rather than putting purchases on a credit card. The theory is that if you see the money leaving your wallet, you'll spend less.

The theory is correct, as several research studies have shown. But it's not exactly using cash that's important—it's the transparency of the payment.

THE LOWER THE TRANSPARENCY, THE MORE PEOPLE SPEND

Payment transparency refers to how tangible the payment is. The more real or tangible a payment is, the more transparent it is. Here's what we know about methods of payment:

- Cash is very tangible. You can touch it and put it in your pocket — it's real—which means you don't like to see it go away. It's very tangible and very transparent.

- Writing a check is a little less transparent than cash, but it's more transparent than credit cards. When you hand over a check, you don't get it back, like cash.

- Credit cards are tangible since there's an actual card, and if you're using it at a store, you do hand over the card, but then the card gets handed back to you, so there isn't a reinforcing sense of loss. Credit cards are less transparent than cash or checks.

- Using a credit card online is even less transparent. If you have your credit card number memorized or if the retailer you're purchasing from has your credit card information stored, then you don't even have to touch the credit card. The transparency is lower than cash or handing over a credit card in a store. You'll likely spend more.

- Amazon's one-click purchasing lowers transparency even further, since all you have to do is click the Buy Now button.

- Subscriptions for products and services where you sign up once and then money is taken from your credit card automatically are less transparent than any of the other methods.

Takeaways

- ☑ If you're a designer working for a company that sells products or services and you want people to spend more money, use the least tangible (least transparent) method possible.

- ☑ Make it easy for people to store payment information.

- ☑ Make it easy for people to use the stored payment method.

- ☑ Build in default payment amounts if possible.

- ☑ Set up your products and services on a subscription basis.

- ☑ Ask people to pay for a subscription once for an entire year instead of billing them monthly.

64 PEOPLE COMMIT TO PURCHASES BECAUSE OF COGNITIVE DISSONANCE

You just bought an expensive pair of shoes. You have a very brief pang of regret. Did you *need* another pair of shoes? Did you need *these* shoes? Should you take them back?

After about 10 seconds, you let go of the regret. "They're great," you say, "and they'll be just right for the wedding I'm going to at the end of the month. It's been a long time since I bought something nice for myself."

You just experienced and overcame cognitive dissonance.

POST-PURCHASE COGNITIVE DISSONANCE

In the mid 1950s, psychologist Leon Festinger (1957) formulated the idea of cognitive dissonance. People like to be consistent in their thoughts and actions. When people act in a way that's inconsistent with their beliefs, when they hold two contradictory beliefs, or when they encounter new information that conflicts with their existing beliefs, then they feel uncomfortable. They'll try to change either their beliefs or actions so that they're cohesive, or consistent, again.

Cognitive dissonance is relevant in many aspects of how people think and behave, and shopping is one. After you make a purchase, you justify it to yourself. If there's anything wrong with the product or service, that may actually strengthen your commitment to the purchase, since feeling that you made a poor choice in the purchase increases your cognitive dissonance.

COGNITIVE DISSONANCE AND RATINGS AND REVIEWS

One way that people can reduce the possibility of cognitive dissonance, or reduce its effects if it occurs, is by telling others what a great purchase they've made. This means that people are more likely to leave a positive review, rating, or testimonial right after they've made a purchase.

Takeaways

☑ The best time to ask for a rating, review, or testimonial is right after a purchase has been made.

☑ To lessen the likelihood of post-purchase cognitive dissonance, send a message to people who have just purchased a product with social validation data—quotes or ratings from others who say how glad they are that they made the purchase.

65 COGNITIVE DISSONANCE MAKES PEOPLE BUY

Research on cognitive dissonance in relation to shopping and purchasing often focuses on the post-purchase reaction. But the studies show that cognitive dissonance is just as relevant, and maybe even more relevant, in the pre-decision process.

In fact, one could argue that marketing and advertising are all about trying to induce a feeling of cognitive dissonance in order to encourage someone to make a purchase. For example, let's say that you have two opposing thoughts, feelings, or ideas:

1. "I'm the kind of person who likes to dress well."

2. "My wardrobe is starting to look dated."

These two thoughts could be contradictory. You'll start to feel conflict because the thoughts are not coherent. According to Festinger's cognitive dissonance theory (1957), you'll want to take action to reduce the conflict. One way to reduce the conflict would be to buy some new clothes (or buy the new pair of shoes).

There are actually two states: dissonance and coherence. Dissonance is when there's a conflict; coherence is when there's no conflict. You might feel dissonance or coherence before or after you make a decision.

In order to remove the uncomfortable feeling of dissonance, you basically have two choices:

1. Take action to remove the conflict (for example, buy the new shoes to update your wardrobe).

2. Change your internal belief about one of the conflicting items ("Actually, I'm not a person who cares much about how I dress" or "My wardrobe isn't really outdated").

When you want to encourage someone to make a purchase, a powerful way to do that is to introduce a conflict and propose the solution for removing the conflict.

CREATING OR HIGHLIGHTING A PROBLEM

One of the ways that cognitive dissonance can be used to encourage buying behavior is to highlight a problem. People may not realize they have a conflict. Advertising or marketing can make people aware that there *is* a problem—and therefore make them aware of a conflict: "I didn't know that eating too much meat puts a strain on the health of the world's environment."

Some would say that sometimes marketing and advertising create a problem where none existed before: "I didn't realize that using the generic brand of shampoo was making my hair dull and lifeless."

Creating and highlighting the problem sets up the cognitive dissonance. Now that you recognize there's a problem or conflict, you'll be uncomfortable. You'll want to reduce that dissonance, and one way to do that will be to purchase the product or service being offered. One role of marketing and advertising is to create messaging that induces pre-decision dissonance and messaging that advocates purchase of a product or service to restore coherence of that particular conflict: "I guess I'm not eating well and I'm overweight, but if I join this gym I can do something about it."

Takeaways

☑ When you want to encourage people to take action, stimulate cognitive dissonance by introducing the idea that they are being inconsistent with their beliefs or behavior. This creates or highlights a problem.

☑ Once you've introduced a conflict, position your service or product to reduce the cognitive dissonance.

66 PEOPLE ARE AFFECTED BY ARBITRARY NUMBERS

Look at the numbers below. Don't actually multiply them—just estimate what you think the answer would be:

1 X 2 X 3 X 4 X 5 X 6 X 7 X 8

Amos Tversky and Daniel Kahneman showed people the numbers the same way I've displayed them above. When they asked people to estimate the product, the average answer was 512. However, if they showed the numbers in the reverse order:

8 X 7 X 6 X 5 X 4 X 3 X 2 X 1

then people estimated that the answer would be 2,250. (The actual answer is 40,320.)

PEOPLE ANCHOR ON NUMBERS

Whatever number people see first affects their perceptions moving forward.

Tversky and Kahneman researched this idea of the effect of numbers in many situations. For example, if a store advertises that soup is on sale, the average number of cans of soup that people will buy is three. But if the store advertises that soup is on sale and that there's a limit of 10 cans per customer, then the average number of cans of soup that people will buy is seven.

Kahneman writes about their experiments in his book *Thinking, Fast and Slow* (2011). People will anchor on a particular number, and that number will affect their reaction (largely unconsciously) to other numbers that appear later, even if the later number has nothing to do with the original numbers.

NUMBER ORDER EFFECTS

This number effect has practical implications for how you display pricing. Let's say that you offer three levels of service. Should the levels be presented in this order:

Silver: $15.99

Gold: $25.99

Platinum: $45.99

Or in this order:

Platinum: $45.99

Gold: $25.99

Silver: $15.99

Tversky and Kahneman's research shows that people are more likely to purchase a more expensive service or product if the higher price is presented first, since they'll anchor on the higher number.

Takeaways

☑ When you want people to spend more, show them high numbers before they get to the point of making a purchase decision. These numbers don't have to be related to the price. You can show the number of people who have purchased your product ("over 10,000 customers") before you show the price of your product ($199).

☑ When ordering prices for products or services, place the higher-priced items at the top of the list. This sets the anchor.

67 ONLINE SHOPPING INCREASES ANTICIPATION

Let's say that you're the CEO of a large retail clothing brand. You have stores through-out the world, and you have a website. People buy shirts, pants, skirts, belts, and so on at your stores and at your site.

If you want people to enjoy the shopping process with your brand, and to be excited about buying your products, what should you do?

Let's say your answer is: "I'm going to make shopping in the stores the best shopping experience possible. We'll have in-store events, models wearing the clothes in the stores, and exciting sales. We'll stock the stores with all colors and sizes, so people can be sure that when they come in, we'll have what they want."

No, not a good answer. I'll give you another try by asking a slightly different question: If people are buying products from your online store, what's the most important thing you can do to get them excited about buying a product from you?

Now you aren't sure what to say. You thought your answer to the first question was great, but then I told you it wasn't. You stumble for a minute and then you light up and say, "We'll give them free overnight shipping!"

Nope, also not a good answer.

EXCITEMENT AND ANTICIPATION

Robert Sapolsky is a neuroscientist who studies dopamine in the brain. He trains monkeys to know that when a light comes on that is a signal. Once the signal arrives (the light comes on), the monkeys know that if they press a button 10 times, after the 10th time, a food treat will appear.

Sapolsky measures the amount and timing of dopamine release in the monkeys' brains during the cycle of signal—pressing—food treat. Figure 67.1 shows the results.

Sapolsky points out that the dopamine release starts as soon as the signal arrives, and ends at the end of the bar pressing. Many people think that dopamine is released when the brain receives a reward, but dopamine is actually released in *anticipation* of a reward. It's the dopamine that keeps the monkeys pressing the bar until the treat arrives.

In the first experiment, the monkeys received the treat as soon as they pressed the bar 10 times. In the second experiment the monkeys received the food treat only 50 percent of the time after they pressed the bar. What happened to the dopamine in that situation? Figure 67.2 shows that twice as much dopamine was released, even though a treat was given only half of the time.

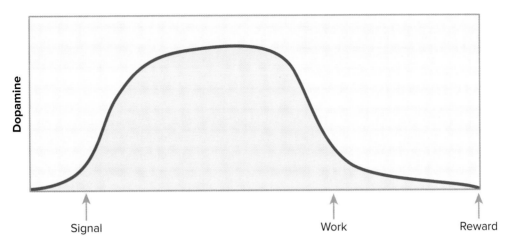

FIGURE 67.1 Dopamine release for monkeys pressing a bar to receive a food treat.

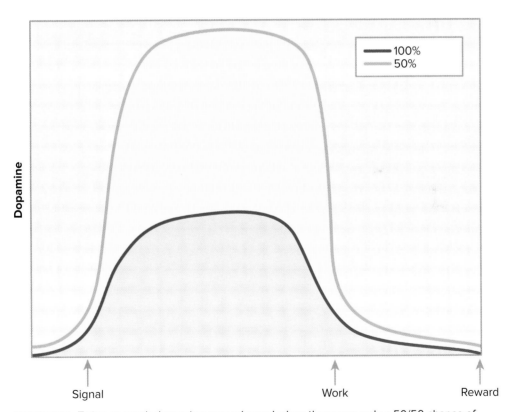

FIGURE 67.2 Twice as much dopamine was released when there was only a 50/50 chance of getting the food treat.

And in the third and fourth experiments, Sapolsky gave the treat 25 percent of the time or 75 percent of the time. Interestingly, when the treat was given either 25 percent of the time or 75 percent of the time, the dopamine release was the same, and it was halfway between the 100 percent and 50 percent chance of getting a food treat.

IT'S ALL ABOUT UNPREDICTABILITY AND ANTICIPATION

When the monkeys got the treat all the time, a fair amount of dopamine was released during the pressing phase. When getting the treat was unpredictable, the amount of dopamine went up. Unpredictability increases anticipation. In the 25- and 75-percent situations, there was actually more predictability. If the monkey got a food treat 25 percent of the time, it meant that they mostly didn't get one. If they got a food treat 75 percent of the time, it meant that they mostly got one. Getting the food treat 50 percent of the time was the least predictable situation.

Figure 67.3 shows what the dopamine chart looked like with the 25-percent and 75-percent condition included.

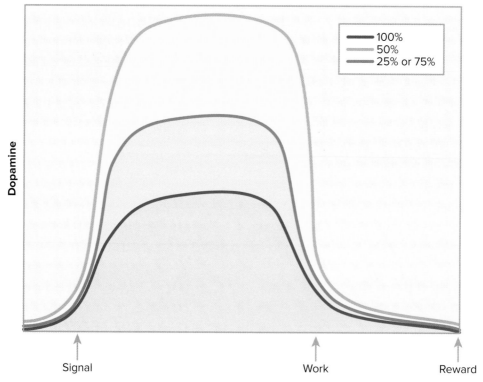

FIGURE 67.3 All three conditions.

Note Sapolsky talks on video about the dopamine—anticipation research at http://www.wired.com/2011/07/sapolsky-on-dopamine-not-about-pleasure-but-its-anticipation/.

ANTICIPATION AND ONLINE SHOPPING

So what do monkeys pressing a bar have to do with online shopping? When people place an order for a product online, they don't get the product right away. They have to wait. And in the waiting is anticipation.

In the report titled *Digital Dopamine* (http://www.razorfish.com/ideas/digital-dopamine.htm), Razorfish presented results from interviews and surveys of 1,680 shoppers from the US, UK, Brazil, and China in 2014. Here's what they found:

> "Seventy-six percent of people in the US, 72 percent in the UK, 73 percent in Brazil, and 82 percent in China say they are more excited when their online purchases arrive in the mail than when they buy things in store."

INSTANT GRATIFICATION ISN'T ALWAYS THE ANSWER

As designers, we tend to think that instant gratification is of the utmost importance. But we should think instead about the entire shopping experience. It's important to find the right spot on the anticipation/instant gratification continuum. If you go too far on the side of instant gratification, then there's no dopamine-fueled anticipation. On the other hand, if you make people wait a really long time, they may be more annoyed with your brand than delighted. People may be willing to wait a lifetime to get into heaven, but they're unlikely to be willing to wait three months for the shirt they ordered without your brand eroding.

WHY FREE OVERNIGHT SHIPPING MAY NOT BE THE ANSWER

I'm aware that when I talk about these issues, some of this is not logical and some online retailers don't agree with me. But remember that these feelings that your customers are having aren't necessarily logical either.

In interviews I conducted about online shopping, I was surprised to discover the following:

- People didn't necessarily want free overnight shipping. They wanted control over when the item(s) would arrive more than they wanted it overnight. For many urban people who didn't have a car, it was especially important for them to be able to control the day and time of the delivery as much as possible.

- People commented on the excitement of waiting for the product to arrive.

- People wanted online shopping to be fun. They weren't just looking for a quick and efficient way to shop.

Takeaways

☑ You can make online shopping as exciting as in-store shopping if you build in anticipation.

☑ Give people as much control as possible over the day and time of delivery of their online purchases.

HOW GENERATIONS, GEOGRAPHY, AND GENDER INFLUENCE DESIGN

There's a lot to think about when you design, and it gets even more complicated when you have to consider the age, gender, or geography of your target audience. In this chapter, you'll find out if and when these three factors are important when you design. For definitional purposes, the US generational definitions are:

Generation Z: Born 1998 to 2013

Millennial Generation: Born 1981 to 1997

Generation X: Born 1965 to 1980

Baby Boom: Born 1946 to 1964

Silent Generation: Born 1928 to 1945

Greatest Generation: Born before 1928

68 EVERYONE USES SMARTPHONES FOR NEWS AND IMPORTANT LIFE EVENTS

Most smartphone owners access news sites sometimes (68 percent), and over a third access news frequently. This holds true across generations.

It may seem like people are using their smartphones to text a friend, check Facebook, or browse the news if they're bored, but according to the Pew Research Center (2014), more than half of the people with smartphones have also used their phones for important tasks:

- 62 percent get information about a health issue
- 57 percent use online banking
- 44 percent look for a place to live

- 40 percent access government services
- 30 percent take a class
- 18 percent apply for a job

People who earn less than $30,000 are almost twice as likely to use a smartphone to look up employment information and four times as likely to apply for a job with their smartphones.

These numbers are even higher for people aged 18 to 29:

- 75 percent get information about a health issue
- 70 percent use online banking

- 44 percent take a class
- 34 percent apply for a job

Takeaways

- ☑ When you provide job listings for lower-income people online, remember that most of them will be accessing the information and applying via a smartphone. Make sure your product is designed to work well with a smartphone.

- ☑ When you provide local or world news or products related to health, banking, employment, or online education, assume that a large percentage of your target audience is accessing your information from a smartphone. Make sure your designs work on a smartphone.

69 GENERATIONAL DIFFERENCES IN SMARTPHONE USE DEPEND ON THE ACTIVITY

The Pew Research Center (2014) conducts surveys on technology use, but it also conducts what it calls an "experience survey." The center contacts people in the study twice a day over a two-week period and asks them which activities they've engaged in over the last hour.

Below are the findings for different age ranges (young = 18–29, middle = 30–49, older = 50+) in the US on different smartphone activities.

Some activities didn't show a lot of generational differences:

- Everyone sent text messages, with not much difference among the ages: 100 percent for the young group, 98 percent for the middle group, and 92 percent for the older group.

- Internet use showed some differences: 97 percent for the young group, 90 percent for the middle group, and 80 percent for the older group.

- Using the phone to make calls was almost the same for everyone: 93 percent for the young group, 91 percent for the middle group, and 94 percent for the older group.

- Emailing was almost the same: 91 percent for the young group, 87 percent for the middle group, and 87 percent for the older group.

But some activities *did* show generational differences:

- Younger people accessed social network sites more than older people: 91 percent for the young group, 77 percent for the middle group, and 55 percent for the older group.

- Younger people watched videos on their smartphones more than older people: 75 percent for the young group, 46 percent for the middle group, and 31 percent for the older group.

- Younger people listened to music on their smartphones more than older people: 64 percent for the young group, 39 percent for the middle group, and 21 percent for the older group.

- Younger people used their smartphones for directions more than older people: 57 percent for the young group, 37 percent for the middle group, and 33 percent for the older group.

- Young people are more likely to use their smartphones to avoid boredom or avoid people than are older people.

Takeaways

☑ If your product is related to social media, video, music, or directions, assume for now that the majority of the people using the product on a smartphone are younger.

☑ If your product is not related to social media, video, or music, don't assume that only younger people are accessing the product on a smartphone.

70 IF THE TASK TAKES LESS THAN 5 MINUTES, PEOPLE WILL USE THEIR SMARTPHONES

According to a survey by Millward Brown Digital (https://www.millwardbrowndigital. com/Research/getting-audiences-right/) of people who own smartphones, if a task is quick (5 minutes), all generations prefer to do the task on a smartphone. But if the task is longer, then all generations prefer to do the task on a laptop or desktop.

But there's a generational difference in the stated reason why they want to switch devices: millennials and baby boomers both say it's because they want a larger screen, while Gen Xers say it's because they want faster speed and performance.

Takeaways

☑ When you're designing a task that's going to take more than 5 minutes to complete, assume that people might not be using a smartphone or may switch from a smartphone to a larger device.

☑ When you're targeting Gen Xers, emphasize the advantage of speed and performance.

☑ When you're targeting millennials or baby boomers, emphasize the advantage of a larger screen.

71 NOT EVERYONE WITH A CELL PHONE HAS A SMARTPHONE

In 2002, 1 in 10 adults in some parts of Africa (Tanzania, Uganda, Kenya, and Ghana) owned a cell phone, according to the Pew Research Center (2015). In 2015, the percentages have grown dramatically, so that in some African countries, 65 percent of adults have a cell phone, and in some countries (South Africa, Nigeria) the percentage is 89 percent (the same as the US).

Most of these phones can text, and in Kenya, Uganda, and Tanzania, mobile banking on cell phones is common.

But only a small percentage of people have smartphones that can access apps and effectively use the Internet. The highest percentages of smartphones in Africa are in South Africa (34 percent) and Nigeria (27 percent).

Younger people, those with more education, and those who speak English are more likely to have smartphones. More men than women own smartphones, except in South Africa, where the percentages are equal.

SHARING PHONES

The most common uses for cell phones in Africa are texting, taking pictures or videos, and transferring money.

Note In Africa, only 3 percent of households have a landline phone. Landline phones never penetrated in Africa. Africa skipped landlines and went straight to cell phones. In contrast, 60 percent of homes in the US have a landline (although the number of US homes without landlines is growing).

Takeaways

- ☑ When you're designing products for Africa, keep in mind that only 34 percent of adults have a smartphone, although that number will continue to rise.

- ☑ Before planning a smartphone app, make sure you understand the smartphone penetration for the countries where your product will be used.

- ☑ When you're designing a product, be mindful of the gender breakdown of smartphone users in the country you're designing for.

72 IN MANY COUNTRIES, WOMEN LACK ONLINE ACCESS

A report by Intel (2012) called "Women and the Web" describes the gap between men and women in online access. Worldwide, the average gap is 25 percent, but that's just the average.

In some countries, such as France and the US, there are as many women as men with online access. In some parts of Europe, women lag behind men when it comes to online access, but just by a few percentage points. In other parts of Europe, the difference between men and women with online access increases to 30 percent. In South Asia, the Middle East, and North Africa, the gap is 35 percent, and in sub-Saharan Africa the difference is as much as 45 percent.

The Intel report lays out the importance of online access for economic mobility through access to information, literacy, and job opportunities, and provides a call to action for governments and philanthropic organizations to help reduce the gap.

Takeaways

☑ When you're designing online products for parts of the world where there's a large gender gap in online access, it's likely that most of your target audience is men.

☑ When you're designing online products for parts of the world where there's a large gender gap in online access, the women who are using your product are likely higher in education and income than many of the other women in that area.

☑ This gender gap will (hopefully) change before too long, so before designing for these parts of the world, check to see if the gap has decreased.

73 GAMERS ARE ALL AGES AND ALL GENDERS

According to a 2014 report from the Entertainment and Software Association, 59 percent of Americans play video games. Of those, 29 percent are under 18 years old, 32 percent are aged 18 to 35, and 39 percent are 36 or older.

In fact, gamers over 65 years old spend more time per day on average playing games than other age groups, perhaps because they have more leisure time.

And in the US, 52 percent of gamers are men and 48 percent are women.

Takeaways

☑ When you're a game designer, don't assume that you're designing your product for a particular age audience, unless you're designing a specialty game (for example, games for children ages 3 to 5). Unless you have data to prove otherwise, assume that gamers are from a wide age range.

☑ When you're designing a story-based game, choose characters and storylines that will be interesting to males and females of all ages.

74 WHAT PEOPLE FIND VISUALLY APPEALING DEPENDS ON AGE, GENDER, AND GEOGRAPHY

Figure 74.1 shows Google and Figure 74.2 shows Naver. Which search engine visual design do you prefer?

FIGURE 74.1 Google search engine home page.

FIGURE 74.2 Naver search engine.

Naver.com is the search engine for South Korea. Google is the search engine for lots of other places. Whether you found the Google design more visually appealing or whether you found the Naver design more visually appealing has a lot to do with how old you are, whether you're a woman or a man, and where you live.

Katharina Reinecke and Krzysztof Gajos (2014) researched different visual designs around the world, with men and women of different ages. Here's what they found:

- People over 40 preferred more colorful designs compared to younger people. This preference was even stronger among people over 50.

- Across all ages, women preferred websites that were more colorful than men did.

- Men preferred websites with a gray or white background and some saturated primary colors.

- Women preferred color schemes with fewer contrasting colors.

- People from Finland, Russia, and Poland liked websites without a lot of colors. People from Malaysia, Chile, and Macedonia preferred websites with a lot of color.

- People from countries near each other tended to like the same amount of colors. For example, Northern European countries didn't like a lot of colors.

- People in English-speaking countries preferred more color than those in Northern European countries.

Takeaways

- ☑ If your target audience is primarily men, consider a white or gray background with a contrasting color.

- ☑ If your target audience is primarily women, consider using more color, but fewer contrasting colors.

- ☑ When you're designing for a specific geographical area, make sure you're familiar with the color and visual design preferences for that region.

- ☑ Test your visual design with your target audience.

- ☑ When you're designing for a geographic area that you're unfamiliar with, be sure to have someone who's familiar with that area on the team to guide you.

75 PEOPLE WANT FEWER CHOICES AS THEY GET OLDER

Andrew Reed researched age differences in preference for the number of choices (2013). Across a variety of different types of decisions, older people preferred fewer choices compared to younger people. The age range was 18 to 90. The lessening in desire for choices was a linear relationship: the older people were, the fewer choices they desired.

Takeaways

☑ When you're designing for younger audiences, offer at least the perception of more choices (remembering that if you give people too many choices, they won't choose anything).

☑ When you're designing for older audiences, you don't have to offer as many choices.

76 THE MENTAL MODEL OF "ONLINE" AND "OFFLINE" IS DIFFERENT FOR DIFFERENT GENERATIONS

Let's say you come over to visit at my house. It's getting dark and I ask you to turn on a lamp that's next to your chair. I phrase the request as, "Would you please turn on the electric lamp?"

You might wonder why I would call it an "electric lamp." Why didn't I just ask you to turn on the lamp?

If you talk to someone who's 55 or older about researching a topic, for example, looking for a recipe that includes eggplant, you're likely to hear them say something like, "I'll go look that up online" or "I'll look that up on the Internet."

If you have the same conversation with someone who's 34 or younger, they're likely to say, "I'll go find a recipe" or "Let me see what I can find."

Adding the word "online" or the phrase "on the Internet" is like saying it's an electric lamp. So what does it matter that the language is a little different? It shows a different mental model of the Internet.

People who grew up before the advent of the Internet think of the Internet as a place to go. It's like going to the library, or going to the store. People who grew up with the Internet don't have that same mental model.

If you have one mental model about the Internet and are designing or writing about products, you're likely to use language that conveys your mental model. That's fine if the people you're designing or writing for have the same mental model that you do. But if they don't, then they'll find parts of your language or your design to be either quaint or confusing.

Takeaways

- ☑ If you're older and designing or writing for younger people, ensure that your language matches the audience. For example, filter out references to "go online" or "on the Internet."

- ☑ If you're younger and designing or writing for older people, be aware that older people have a different mental model. Make sure to test your designs, labels, and instructions with people who are older to make sure your mental model hasn't caused confusion in your design or language.

77 OVER HALF OF THE PEOPLE OVER AGE 65 IN THE US USE THE INTERNET

The Pew Research Center (2015) has been collecting data on Internet use in the US since 2000. Comparing the data from 2000 to 2015, the center reports the following generational changes:

- Overall, 84 percent of American adults use the Internet, compared to 52 percent in the year 2000, but this varies according to different subgroups. In 2000, only 14 percent of people aged 65 or older used the Internet, but in 2015 the number is 58 percent. For the 50 to 64 age group, the numbers went from 46 percent in 2000 to 81 percent in 2015.

- The same pattern holds for younger people. In 2000, 61 percent of people aged 30 to 49 used the Internet. In 2015, the number is 93 percent. And for people in the 18 to 29 age group, the percentage has grown from 70 percent in 2000 to 96 percent in 2015.

NOT A REAL SURPRISE

The more money you make, the more likely you are to use the Internet. The more education you have, the more likely you are to use the Internet. And if you live in a rural area, you're less likely to use the Internet.

NO GENDER DIFFERENCES FOR USE IN THE US

Many people think that use of the Internet is higher among men than women, but that wasn't really true in 2000: 54 percent of men versus 50 percent of women used the Internet. And it definitely isn't true now: 85 percent of men versus 84 percent of women use the Internet today.

Takeaways

☑ Don't assume that you're designing your product primarily for younger people unless your own research shows that's true.

☑ Unless you're designing an age-specific product, assume that people of many ages will use the product.

☑ Be careful when making age-related decisions. For example, make sure the ages of people in photos resonate with your audience, and don't use fonts that might be too small for older users to read.

78 PEOPLE OVER 40 HAVE PRESBYOPIA

Presbyopia is often called farsightedness. Starting at age 40, the eyes lose the ability to focus on objects that are nearby. This is because the lens of the eye starts to harden. Presbyopia starts sometime after 40 and gets worse until about age 65 when it stays, but stabilizes.

If you're under 40, it's hard to imagine what this is really like. But if you know people over 40, you've probably noticed that they start holding anything they're trying to read farther and farther away.

Presbyopia can be corrected with glasses. People with other vision problems who already have glasses often end up getting bi- or tri-focal glasses after 40.

Presbyopia often remains a problem, however, for people who are using screens.

To help people with presbyopia, let them make the text larger (for example, on a Kindle) on their own. If they can't, and if your application or product is for people over age 40, consider using at least a 16-point font size.

Note According to the International Centre for Eyecare Education in South Africa, more than 1 billion people globally have presbyopia.

Takeaways

☑ When you can, let people enlarge the text when they're viewing your product.

☑ When you're designing a product primarily for people over age 40, consider using what will seem like a very large font to you (if you're under 40), for example, a 16-point font size.

☑ Test your product on people with presbyopia to make sure they can see and read what they need to.

79 THE COLOR BLUE FADES WITH AGE

Another type of vision issue that occurs when people get older is that their color vision declines. It becomes harder to distinguish colors that are similar and the color blue becomes faded.

It's not a good idea, therefore, to use the color blue as a code, and even worse to use blue and similar colors to give meaning. For example, if you showed a map with different colors to delineate the spread of the flu virus—where blue means widespread reporting of flu, blue/green means medium-level reports, and so on—older people might find it hard to distinguish the colors.

Takeaways

- ☑ Avoid using the color blue as a means of providing information.

- ☑ When you're showing areas of color to give meaning, use colors that are very different from each other.

- ☑ Make sure you have lots of contrast between the foreground (for example, the text) and the background.

80 NEARLY 100 MILLION PEOPLE OVER AGE 65 HAVE HEARING PROBLEMS

A total of 360 million people globally have hearing problems, and one-quarter of those (90 million) are over age 65.

If you're designing a product that has an auditory component, be mindful that not everyone will be able to hear it. This is especially problematic if you have audio or video that's critical to using your product.

Make sure people can control the audio levels, and consider captioning your content.

Takeaways

☑ Five percent of the people in the world have hearing problems, and that number increases if your target audience is older.

☑ Consider using captioning for your audio and video files so that text transcripts are available for people with hearing problems.

☑ Provide people with as much volume control as possible.

81 MOTOR SKILLS DON'T DECLINE UNTIL THE MID-60S

Unlike vision, motor skills don't decline until the mid-60s. (One exception is if you have a disease that affects motor skills, such as Parkinson's.)

Priscila Caçola (2013) tested young, middle-aged, and older (over 65) people. She had them perform various fine motor movements, including finger tapping, while having to recognize and order numbers. She tested people in three levels of complexity.

There were no differences between the young and middle-aged participants, but they both performed faster than the older group.

The good news is that the decline wasn't until people were in their mid-60s. Unlike vision decline, motor decline starts later.

So much of technology use requires fine motor tasks: moving and clicking with a mouse, using a track pad, touching and swiping a smartphone. Many people over age 65 will start to have problems using technology because of motor decline.

Takeaways

☑ When your target audience includes people over 65, be aware that motor movements become more difficult at that age. If possible, build in voice interactions so people don't have to do as much fine motor manipulation.

☑ Don't assume that older people are taking longer to complete a task because they aren't thinking as fast. It might be more motor control than cognitive ability.

☑ Leave space between things on a screen that people have to hit as a target either with their mouse or finger to reduce accidental selecting.

☑ The larger the target, the easier it is to hit. Make buttons at least 9.6 mm diagonal measurement and maybe even larger if you have a primarily older target audience.

82 OLDER PEOPLE MAY NOT HAVE ANSWERS TO THOSE SECURITY QUESTIONS

Jim is 70 years old. He's setting up an account to listen to music with an online music app. He's on the security screen and the form asks him to pick security questions to set up an account and type in the answers. He has to pick two questions from the following choices:

- Who was your third-grade teacher?

- What was the name of the first school you attended?

- What was the name of your first pet?

- What is your father's birthdate?

- What street did you live on when you were born?

- Who was your best friend in high school?

- What was your nickname as a child?

To the 27-year-old who created this set of security questions, these sound like reasonable questions. After all, the user only has to pick two of them. Certainly two of them have to work for everyone, right?

I DON'T HAVE ANSWERS TO ANY OF THE QUESTIONS

I'm younger than Jim, and I don't have answers for any of the questions. I moved a lot when I was young. I lived in the apartment where I was born for three months. I attended 12 schools before I graduated from high school. My parents died when I was young, so I don't remember their birthdates. I would have a hard time coming up with two questions out of the set above that I had actual answers to.

For someone who's older than I am, it's even worse. For Jim, who is 70, it's been over 50 years since he had his first car, and he's had dozens since then. It's been 62 years since he was in third grade. It's been 70 years since he was born. It's unlikely that someone who is 70 would know the answers to two of these questions.

Even if Jim had a great memory he might not have answers to these questions. Maybe he (and I) could just make up some answers. But the problem with making up answers is that we won't remember them. (I've tried doing this.) Just write them down, then, right? But isn't the idea of security questions that you wouldn't have them written down somewhere where people can find them?

Takeaways

☑ Don't ask people to remember information from many years ago.

☑ Don't ask security questions that require long-term memory.

83 AS PEOPLE AGE, THEY BECOME LESS CONFIDENT ABOUT THEIR OWN MEMORIES

If I told you that as people age their neuroplasticity declines—as they get older, they're less able to learn new things, create new neuronal connections, and retrieve memories—you'd probably nod and say, yes, you've heard that's true. It's a piece of conventional wisdom that everyone seems to know and seems to think makes sense. Except that it's not true!

Dayna Touron (2015) has researched memory in older adults and found that memory often does not decline as much as everyone thinks, but that older adults aren't confident in their ability to make new memories or retrieve old ones.

When Touron had people learn a new route with a GPS device, the younger adults learned the route and then stopped using the GPS much faster than the older adults. It's not because the older adults took longer to commit the route to memory. It turns out that the adults between ages 60 and 75 hesitated to give up the GPS and rely instead on what they've learned.

Touron has found this reluctance to trust one's own memory to be true of older adults in many different situations and contexts, including verbal tasks (recognizing word pairs) and mathematical tasks (solving equations). In the mathematical tasks, older adults went over the same calculations many times rather than relying on their memory of how to solve the equations.

Interestingly, if she offered a small cash prize in return for a quick answer, then they did rely on their memory.

Touron believes that older adults aren't confident in their memory abilities, and so will stick with other methods even if they're inefficient. She also believes that older adults underestimate just how inefficient they're being, don't think that using their memories will be much of a shortcut, and don't believe their memories are entirely accurate.

This lack of confidence in memory may be why older adults take longer to do tasks with technology than younger adults. We tend to think it's because they think more slowly, or their memories are poor. It may actually be that they don't have confidence in their ability to make new memories or retrieve old ones.

Takeaways

☑ Assume that older adults may take longer to complete some tasks.

☑ Encourage older adults to use their memory of how to do something rather than follow instructions.

84 GENERATION Z WILL ACCOUNT FOR 40 PERCENT OF ALL CONSUMERS IN 2020

If you were born after 1965, then you might still be trying to figure out the Millennial generation. I suggest you forget about that and move right to figuring out Generation Z.

Generation Z includes people born between 1998 and 2013. Here are some things to know about Generation Z:

- They make up approximately 25 percent of the population worldwide, which means there are 1.8 billion Generation Zers in the world, and 80 million of them in the US.

- Although they're 25 percent by population, that percentage will grow (as older generations die), and by 2020 Generation Z will be 40 percent of consumers.

- Generation Zers are very social online, but they're not frequent users of Facebook.

Takeaways

☑ When you're designing a product for the general adult population and you expect it to last for more than two or three years, include Generation Z in your target audience.

☑ If you're not familiar with Generation Z, you should be. Conduct target audience research with Generation Z *now*.

☑ When you're designing for Generation Z, test your product with them before you go live.

85 MORE THAN ONE-THIRD OF 1-YEAR-OLDS CAN USE A TOUCH SCREEN

Hilda Kabali (2015) researched the use of various screen devices by babies and toddlers with a survey of the parents of patients at the Einstein Medical Center pediatric clinic in Philadelphia. The clinic serves an urban, low-income, minority community. The children were from 0 to 4 years old. Most of the homes had multiple technologies:

- TV (97 percent)
- Tablets (83 percent)
- Smartphones (77 percent)
- Internet access (59 percent)

Here are some of the survey results:

- 36 percent of babies had swiped a touch screen before they were 1 year old, and 24 percent had called someone on a smartphone.

- 36 percent of the babies had played a video game and used an app before they were 2 years old.

- By the age of 4, 38 percent of the children were using a mobile or tablet device for at least an hour a day.

Note Some therapists in the UK now have special digital addiction rehab programs for young children who show signs of addiction to electronic devices.

Takeaways

- ☑ The age of target audiences is getting younger and younger.

- ☑ If you haven't been asked to design for very young children, you may be asked before too long.

- ☑ When you design for young children, you have two target audiences—the young children and their parents—because the parents of very young children make the purchase/use decision initially. Make sure you're designing for both.

- ☑ Test your designs with both children and their parents.

86 WHEN TODDLERS LAUGH, THEY LEARN MORE

Let's say you decide to let your 18-month-old daughter play some learning games on your tablet. You have a couple of apps you've downloaded and you're trying to decide which one to give to her: The one that introduces number and letter concepts with music but is pretty serious? Or the one that makes her laugh with the silly animals that keep popping up and running around the screen?

Since you're not sure that "screen time" is a good thing for young children, you choose the serious one. At least she'll learn, you think.

Actually, the one that makes her laugh is the better decision.

Rana Esseily (2015) conducted research on babies as young as 18 months old. There are many research studies that show that when children laugh, it enhances their attention, motivation, perception, memory, and learning. But this study was the first to try out the idea on children as young as 18 months old.

The children in the group who did a task in a way that made them laugh learned the target actions more than those in the control group who were not laughing during the learning period.

Note The researcher hypothesizes that laughter may help with learning because dopamine released while laughing enhances learning.

Takeaways

☑ When you're designing learning apps or products for children, include plenty of opportunities to get the children to laugh.

☑ You may need to include messaging to the parents about the research that shows that laughing enhances learning.

☑ Make sure you test your apps with children in the target age range. What makes you laugh may or may not make them laugh.

HOW PEOPLE INTERACT WITH INTERFACES AND DEVICES

For decades, the main way that people interacted with computers and technology devices has been with screens and keyboards, mice and trackpads, and maybe sometimes with pens or fingers or voices. Now the devices are changing and the input is changing. This chapter covers how people interact with devices and controls that they're used to and how they interact with the new devices just coming on the market or that are soon to arrive.

87 PEOPLE WANT TO SKIM AND SCAN VIDEOS

Video has become such an important medium online, yet video interface design is given surprisingly little attention. We have special devices and software for presenting text and images, but it seems we think of videos as being something we embed on a page, but can't alter in any way to make it more usable.

Researchers at the University of California at Berkeley have been rethinking that assumption.

When a video is short—2 to 3 minutes—it probably makes sense to just watch it from beginning to end. But what if the video is 20 minutes long, or an hour, for example, a conference talk or an online course?

Up to now it's been very unusual to be able to browse, scan, and skim the content of a video. So the team at UC Berkeley came up with the idea of a video digest.

A video digest is a way to partition a long video into chapters and sections within a chapter. For each segment and chapter, you can read a short summary about that part of the video, and see a thumbnail. It means that, as a user, you can skim through a video and even click on the thumbnail and watch that part of the video. All of this is created post-production, meaning that existing videos can be turned into digests.

Figure 87.1 shows what the interface looks like.

FIGURE 87.1 The Video Digest interface.

The team has also created a tool that anyone can use to create the digests. With the software tool you can:

1. Manually create chapters, sections, text summaries, and thumbnails.

2. Have the tool create chapters, sections, text summaries, and thumbnails.

3. Have the tool create chapters, sections, text summaries, and thumbnails, and then manually adjust them.

Options 1 and 3 provide more useful digests, but even having the tool produce a digest is better than no digest at all.

Check out the video-digest authoring tool at http://vis.berkeley.edu/videodigests.

Takeaways

☑ When you provide a video that's longer than 5 minutes, offer a video digest to make the video more usable.

☑ Creating a digest manually is best, but even a digest created algorithmically is better than no digest at all.

88 PEOPLE INTERACT WITH CAROUSELS

To carousel or not to carousel. Is that the question?

First, let's review what a carousel is. A carousel is an interface element, typically used at websites, that shows a large image and then either automatically, or with a user click or swipe, shows another large image and so on, showing essentially a "gallery" of images in a row.

I'm aware that I'm going against the grain in asserting that people interact with carousels. Many designers hate carousels and some like to use them. No matter which one you are, I hope you can set aside your own feelings about carousels to read some of the data below.

People love to hate carousels. In a July 8, 2013, blog post, Erik Runyon offered some data on carousels that are used on the University of Notre Dame website, ND.edu (http://erikrunyon.com/2013/07/carousel-interaction-stats/):

On the ND.edu home page carousel, visitors clicked the first picture of the carousel quite frequently (for example, 89 percent), but rarely clicked the pictures in the other positions in the carousel (picture 2: 3 percent, picture 3: 2 percent, and so on).

For a departmental site at ND.edu, the pattern was similar, but not as severe—visitors clicked the first picture of the carousel quite frequently (for example, 71 percent, position 2: 7 percent, and so on).

But for a news site at ND.edu, the pattern was quite different. Visitors clicked the first picture of the carousel 55 percent, the second picture 18 percent, the next picture 11 percent, and so on.

Runyon reports on the data from a few other carousels at other parts of the ND.edu website, and they vary as the ones above do.

BUT WAIT, THERE'S MORE

Before you try to draw conclusions, here's more data. In a February 9, 2015, blog post, Kyle Peatt talks about the Runyon blog and presents some data of his own (http://www.smashingmagazine.com/2015/02/09/carousel-usage-exploration-on-mobile-e-commerce-websites/#luke-carousels).

Here are some of Peatt's points:

- Peatt says that Runyon's data is based the measurement of clicking, and that it should instead be based on whether the visitor interacts in any way. When Peatt analyzes his own data using any interaction instead of just clicks, then the interaction rate for the carousels at his test sites goes from 23 percent up to 72 percent. Users were often advancing the carousel instead of clicking or tapping, and he says that should count too.

- Specifically, Peatt says any interaction, including swiping on a smartphone, clicking an arrow to advance or reverse the carousel, tapping a thumbnail at the bottom of the carousel, or tapping on the slide to zoom the image into a full-screen view should all count as interaction. And if they do, then data shows that carousels are often effective at engaging visitors.

- Peatt makes the point that the context and content of the carousels is important too. Carousels at e-commerce websites, where interacting with the carousel gives the visitor more information on products, results in fairly high interaction rates. If the content of the carousel is not interesting, useful, or compelling, then people don't interact with it.

- One of the criticisms of carousels is that if people don't interact with them, they're really just big pictures on the page. Peatt's comment about that is, essentially, "So what? What's wrong with having a big picture on the page?"

- One of the biggest problems with carousels that Peatt addresses is the problem of accessibility. Most carousel implementations can't be read by the screen readers that are used by people with visual impairments.

Takeaways

☑ Not all carousels are bad. Don't dismiss them out of hand in your designs.

☑ The accessibility issue is probably the biggest reason to use carousels with caution.

☑ If you're providing useful images that relate to the purpose of visiting the website, carousels can engage people and people will interact with them.

89 PEOPLE SCROLL

For quite awhile there has been a back and forth in interface design about whether scrolling is a "good" or usable choice. If you have a lot of information or content on a page, should you present it all on one page and have people scroll? Or should you break it up into multiple pages and have people move forward through pages?

One rule of thumb in online design is that if it's important, it should go above the fold—that is, if you require people to scroll past the fold, they won't, and therefore information below the fold won't be seen. Is this true?

Note The term "the fold" comes from newspaper design. When a newspaper is folded in half, there's text above the fold and text below the fold. Online there's the same concept, but "above the fold" refers to what people can see on the screen without having to scroll.

Chartbeat analyzed data from 2 billion website visits and found that 66 percent of the visits' time were spent below the fold; in other words, visitors had scrolled.

ClickTale analyzed 100,000 visits to websites and reported that people scrolled on 76 percent of the pages and went all the way to the bottom on 22 percent of the pages.

Note People are used to vertical scrolling, but horizontal scrolling is still a bad idea. (I'm distinguishing between a swipe and a scroll.) Horizontal swipes are much easier to perform than horizontal scrolls.

Takeaways

☑ It's all right to create a page that requires vertical scrolling.

☑ Avoid horizontal scrolling. But horizontal swiping is OK.

☑ Even though people will scroll, make sure to put your most important information above the fold.

☑ To encourage scrolling, keep showing great and useful content.

☑ Avoid "dead zones," places that are so uninteresting that people tend not to scroll any further.

90 PEOPLE CAN'T EVEN TALK TO THE CAR WHILE DRIVING

People know that they shouldn't be using their smartphones while driving, yet they still do it. But what about talking to their cars while driving?

Bryan Reimer (2015) wanted to know if a newer, cloud-based speech recognition system on a smartphone (specifically, the Samsung Galaxy S4) would be easier to use and cause less driving disruption when placing calls or getting navigation directions than an embedded vehicle voice system.

He tested 80 people with good driving records and had them use the Samsung smartphone (mounted on the dash and with the sound coming through a Bluetooth interface into the car's embedded system) and then either a Chevrolet Equinox with MyLink or a Volvo XC60 with Sensus.

The participants drove on a highway at the normal highway speed and called people from their contact list as well as entered an address to get directions.

Reimer measured task demand, including heart rate, skin conductance, and self-reporting. He also measured visual engagement and driving performance. Participants would call a phone number with the phone by using the screen as well as using the voice interface. Entering the address was only by voice.

Reimer's hypothesis was that there would be fewer errors and less task demand with the smartphone. Here's what he discovered:

- Voice methods had less task demand than manual methods, both for the smartphone as well as the embedded system.

- For making a phone call to a contact, task demand was less with the embedded system than with the cell phone. Reimer notes that the cell phone was mounted. In some ways, he thinks that might have made it safer since the person wasn't holding the phone. On the other hand, he mentions that because the smartphone was mounted, the voice recognition might not have been ideal. Having to reach to touch small icons on the phone may have added to the task demand for the smartphone condition.

- When it came to entering an address for directions, however, people spent more time with their eyes off the road while talking to the embedded system than while talking to the smartphone. The Chevrolet Equinox had the most errors. Reimer tested the ambient noise level and it was much higher in the Equinox. This, he says, may be part of the reason that there were more errors with the Equinox embedded system on this task.

Takeaways

☑ Learn voice interface design. More and more apps will use it. Designers need to know how to design for voice, not just for screen displays.

☑ Take ambient noise into account. Learn about the environments where people are using your app, and how much ambient noise you should account for.

91 PEOPLE DON'T ALWAYS ENGAGE MORE WHEN YOU'VE USED "GAMIFICATION"

Sometimes clients call me with specific requests: "We want to make our website more engaging," or "We want to increase conversions." Everyone now and then someone will say, "We want to add gamification." That one is a red flag for me.

Gamification refers to using elements of game playing and game design in the design of a non-game product, such as a website, software, or application, for example, using gamification to make an HR intranet more interesting, or to make an e-commerce site more engaging.

As of 2012, articles started appearing about how gamification wasn't working. It wasn't living up to its promise. Reasons given were that people were tired of it, or that the expectations of the companies that were using it were too high.

Those reasons might add to the problem, but they aren't the most important reasons why gamification isn't working outside of games.

The problem lies in what the companies meant by gamification and what they actually implemented. There are three main problems:

1. Most of the implementation of games in non-game settings seems to center around competition and rewards. Certainly both competition and rewards can be part of a gamification strategy, but they're just two strategies, and they aren't even the most powerful. More motivating than competition and reward are things such as:

   - Stories. Many games include a story/plotline, and compelling characters to identify with.

   - Desire for mastery. Most games stimulate the intrinsic desire to learn new skills and knowledge.

   - Need to belong. Part of the motivation of playing a game can be the fact that you're part of a community of people who also play that game.

   These are intrinsic motivators. Rewards are extrinsic motivators. Most of the time, intrinsic motivators are more powerful and effective than extrinsic motivators.

2. Many of the gamification attempts I see miss one or more of the important motivators above, and they implement them poorly even when they think to use them. For example, if you're going to stimulate the desire for mastery, you must do the following:

- Give people autonomy. When people feel they have control over what they do and how and when they do it, the desire for mastery is stimulated.

- Provide clear feedback. Feedback doesn't mean, "Hey, you're doing great!" That's not feedback. That's praise. If you want to stimulate the desire for mastery, you need to give feedback without praise. (You'll find out why in a moment). Feedback lets people know that what they did was correct because it made something happen.

- Provide the right amount of challenge. If the task is too difficult, it won't stimulate the desire for mastery. But if the task is too easy, it won't stimulate it either.

3. Using rewards in particular tends to counteract the desire for mastery. So sometimes giving a reward (even praise) can actually cause a reduction in engagement. Yet rewards seem to be the most common (sometimes the only) technique that's applied when people talk about gamification of non-game products.

Takeaways

☑ When you implement gamification, use multiple motivators.

☑ Before you add rewards, consider building in intrinsic motivators such as stories, the desire for mastery, and the need to belong.

---

92 GAMES CAN IMPROVE PERCEPTUAL LEARNING

When my son was about 6 years old, we were shopping in Target. He saw a group of 10-to 13-year-olds playing video games on the demo machines, and was fascinated (video games were not part of his life at that time), so he stopped to watch. Not wanting him to get too interested, and also being in a rush to get my shopping done, I said something like, "You don't want to play video games. It's scrambling their brains." I started walking to the checkout lanes and then realized he hadn't followed me. I turned back to where he was standing at the video game section and found him staring intently at one of the boys playing the video games. "What are you doing?" I asked. My son turned to me and said thoughtfully, "He doesn't look like his brains are scrambled."

I was pretty strict with my children about video games. We never owned a game console, and I limited their video game time to "educational" games. My daughter never did become a fan, but my son did when he went off to college and beyond.

Now, looking at the research, I realize I may have been wrong about video games.

VIDEO GAMES CAN INCREASE PERCEPTUAL LEARNING

Some of you may be parents who appreciate video games, and others may be parents like I was, who thought that video games were not a good way for children to spend time. Research shows that playing video games isn't necessarily a bad thing. There are benefits: training in action video games can increase the speed of perceptual processing and something called perceptual learning. It's possible to train the senses—vision, hearing, motor skills—and improve their capabilities, especially with action games.

When people play video games, it can increase how quickly they're able to process sensory stimuli. It can increase the ability to filter out extraneous sensory stimuli and focus on one perceptual channel.

Brian Glass (2013) cites research studies showing that when people who are new to video games are taught how to play action games, they can process visual information faster as a result, even outside of the gaming context.

EVEN ADULTS CAN CREATE NEW NEURON STRUCTURES

For many decades, it was assumed that the brain has the most flexibility and neurons at birth and that it's basically downhill from there. There's the old adage about not consuming too much alcohol, lest it kill the finite number of brain cells you have. Along with this idea came the theory that brain structures become more rigid over time—that as people get older, their brains can't be rewired. This has all turned out to be untrue. The adult brain has neuroplasticity—its neural structures can change and keep changing and learning. The skills learned from video gaming are an example of neuroplasticity.

STRATEGY GAMES INCREASE COGNITIVE FLEXIBILITY

In addition to the perceptual learning that action video games provide, research shows that strategy games (think StarCraft) can also improve cognitive flexibility. Cognitive flexibility is the ability to coordinate four things:

1. What you're paying attention to

2. What you're thinking about

3. What rules to use

4. How to make a decision

The more cognitively flexible you are, the higher your intelligence and psychological health.

COGNITIVE FLEXIBILITY IS TRAINABLE

Glass took women who were not gamers and had them play games for an hour a day for 40 days. One group played Sims 2, another played StarCraft with one base, and the third group played StarCraft with two bases at different locations. Cognitive flexibility was measured before and after the training. The two groups playing StarCraft raised their cognitive flexibility scores more than the group that played Sims 2. And the group that managed two bases increased even more than the group that managed one base.

Takeaways

☑ If you don't play video games, you might want to try some to improve your own flexibility.

☑ Being a game designer requires a special set of skills. If you're interested in becoming a game designer, you'll need to take some courses to get up to speed.

☑ If you're a game designer or planning to become one, look for opportunities to include perceptual learning and/or cognitive flexibility in your games.

☑ Consider building in intrinsic motivators such as stories, the desire for mastery, and the need to belong before you add rewards.

93 PEOPLE NEED FEWER CHOICES

The research is clear that people like having a lot of choices, but that providing a lot of choices not only makes it harder for them to take action, but may also induce stress.

Designers often make decisions based on preference, not performance. Many designs inundate the target audience with choices.

For example, a search for an external hard drive on Amazon brings back 21,287 results. According to the Huffington Post, Starbucks has said there are over 80,000 choices you can make in ordering a beverage.

Can we design so that we eliminate choices? According to Aaron Shapiro, CEO of Huge, the answer is yes. Shapiro wrote about this idea, called anticipatory design in *Fast Company* (http://www.fastcodesign.com/3045039/the-next-big-thing-in-design-fewer-choices).

REMOVING UNNECESSARY CHOICES

Anticipatory design is built on a few key ideas:

1. Too many choices leads to poor decisions.

2. Many, if not most, choices are unnecessary.

3. Design can eliminate unnecessary choices.

This brings up an interesting question: Is the role of the designer to present the user with all the choices in the easiest possible way for the user to digest and act? Or is the role of the designer to anticipate what choices are really relevant and present only those? Anticipatory design advocates would say the latter is correct. Even more, anticipatory design is about making and implementing decisions for the user—automatically, and without user input. The goal is not to help the user make a decision, but to anticipate what the user needs and just do it.

Radical, yes?

Note In the 1950s, Buckminster Fuller taught a course at MIT about anticipatory design—a concept he developed in 1927—but it really means something different. However, if you search online for the term "anticipatory design," you'll likely encounter Fuller's version of the term.

GOING BEYOND PERSONALIZATION

Aren't we already doing this when we personalize and customize? My Netflix account recommends movies for me. My weather app knows what cities I usually look up weather for and shows those automatically. Isn't that anticipatory design? No, that's just a baby step according to Shapiro.

HERE'S YOUR COFFEE YOU DIDN'T ORDER

When I go to Starbucks, I order the same beverage almost all of the time. What if Starbucks could tell via GPS that I was close, and send me a text:

We are preparing your:

Tall, decaf, latte with skim milk

To be ready in 5 minutes

To be charged to your credit card...

To accept this order, press Accept. To change the order, press Change. To cancel the order, press Cancel.

Anticipatory design doesn't mean you decide what people want. It means doing enough research that you're confident that you know what their decisions will be—and then delivering that. It's not easy, but it is possible. This will take some work to implement successfully, technically behind the scenes, as well as with designers and users. But it might very well be worth it.

Takeaways

☑ **Rethink your role as designer. What would you do differently if your role were to relieve the user from making as many decisions as possible?**

☑ **Try out anticipatory design.**

---

94 PEOPLE WANT DEVICES TO MONITOR THEIR HEALTH

People like having control, including control over their own bodies. This is part of the reason for the popularity of devices that, without being implanted, let people get a read on what's going on inside their bodies. Here are some of the first devices that were developed:

- MyTensio, a wireless cuff that monitors your blood pressure over a period of time

- Lethal, a device you put in your shoe that vibrates to give you haptic data for directions and collects data on your activity level. It can also be used to help the visually impaired navigate.

- Skulpt Aim, which measures muscle density and fat percentage and sends the info to your smartphone

- Vital Connect, a wearable patch that collects data on your heart rate and temperature

- Smart contact lenses, created by Google for people with diabetes, measure glucose in your tears and let you know when it's time to take your insulin.

- June, a bracelet that measures your exposure to sun, sends the data to your smartphone, and gives you advice about the sunscreen you should be wearing

- FitBark, which you can put on your dog's collar to track its activities

These devices incorporate multiple types of design. There's the design of the device itself, the design of the user experience on the device, and the design of the user experience for what the device talks to (for example, a smartphone app).

Industrial designers are skilled at designing the physical form of the device, and mobile designers should be able to handle the smartphone part, but the design of the interface on the wearable itself often has usability issues. Designing something with a small screen requires a different set of skills. Designers tend to go into "mode" mindset. It takes a lot of skill to create a usable modal interface, as evidenced by all the impossible-to-use watch interfaces.

Takeaways

☑ As the demand for wearable well-being devices increases, more designers will be needed—especially designers who know how to design very small device interfaces.

☑ There will likely be opportunities to work in this arena, so if you're interested in being a wearable interface designer, you might want to start now. Create a proto-type interface for a pretend wellness wearable so you can get a sense of what this type of design is like.

☑ To design for small wearables that consumers will interact with directly, conduct user research to understand the context of use and the most important or frequent tasks so you can design for those first.

95 PEOPLE WILL INCREASINGLY HAVE DEVICES IMPLANTED TO MONITOR AND INTERVENE IN THEIR HEALTH

In the 1970s, on US TV, there was a show called *The Six Million Dollar Man.* The premise is that an astronaut is in an aircraft accident and one arm, both legs, and one eye—being beyond repair—are replaced with bionic implants. These give him special powers (he can run almost 100 km/h for example).

Today's bionic implants and wearables don't necessarily give people special powers, but we are seeing a huge increase in the merging of biological with non-biological, and biological with technology.

In the US, 2.5 million people already have a medical device implanted in their bodies. These include pacemakers, defibrillators, and cochlear implants.

These days the implanted devices can communicate information from the body out to the individual, or to the person's medical team.

And medical teams can go the other way. The devices can be wirelessly programmed or given instructions to take a certain action (such as giving a shock to a heart that is beating erratically).

Designing these (and other) medical devices requires some additional skills and knowledge from designing other technology products. Here are some things you will encounter:

In many countries (including the US), there are special government requirements for designing medical devices. In the US, for example, the FDA regulates medical devices. They must be designed and developed following special processes, for example, designing the input and output, having a formal design review, verifying the design, validating the design, keeping a formal Design History file, and so on. (A background in user-centered design will be very helpful.)

Medical devices are often implanted and used in contexts that have to be taken into account during design. For example, devices may need to be programmed during surgery. Operating theaters often have unusual lighting. There may be stress or time constraints, which means that decisions must be made quickly. I was once working with a medical device design team that had included printing something out on a printer as part of the workflow. When I did some environment/context research, I discovered that the printer was a good 60-second walk from where the product would be used.

Takeaways

☑ If you're part of a medical device design team, make sure some of the people on the team have designed medical devices before.

☑ Context is always important, but if you're designing a medical device, pay special attention to the environment and context of use in your design decisions.

☑ Familiarize yourself with the rules of medical device design in the country you live in or are designing for.

96 PEOPLE CAN CONTROL TECHNOLOGY WITH THEIR BRAINS

It's somewhat easy to understand that people would be willing to have a medical device implanted in order to control or monitor critical health functioning, but what about having a brain implant so you can control your devices, such as your smartphone and computer? Or what if your brain were hardwired right into the Internet, so that when you thought of a question, the answer appeared in your brain automatically from Google?

If you think this is out of the realm of possibility, think again.

A brain implant (often called a neural implant) is the size of an aspirin and is placed right under your skull. It's a relatively fast and easy procedure. Once the implant is there, it can send and receive signals.

Note The Defense Advanced Research Projects Agency (DARPA) is part of the US Department of Defense, and develops technologies for the US military. DARPA is working on a project called Systems-Based Neurotechnology for Emerging Therapies (SUBNETS). SUBNETS will monitor brain signals of soldiers through a brain implant. The data will be analyzed and the brain implant could then be used to alter the electrical activity of the brain to intervene in mood disorders and depression.

MIND READING?

There are plenty of things to think about with this technology. Already, devices can monitor your brain waves and determine what letter of the alphabet you're thinking about or whose face you're imagining. Do you want to have an ad for a restaurant appear in your thoughts because some machine picked up on the fact that you were thinking about food?

Do you have to worry about someone hacking your brain?

Note If you don't want a brain implant, you can still control a computer with your brain. Using a device such as a NeuroSky headset, you can think what you want to do and your brain signals are communicated through wifi. An example is using the NeuroSky to change stations on a TV, or play games.

Takeaways

☑ Like it or not, brain-machine interfaces have arrived. Designers will have to decide if they want to participate in this early stage or not.

☑ If you're interested in developing for this audience, pick up one of the available headset products. They are reasonably priced and some of them come with technology so you can build your own apps.

97 PEOPLE WILL ADAPT TO MULTI-MODAL INTERFACES

When I travel I can handle a little bit of museum time, but a museum is usually not my first choice of how to spend an entire day.

So I was surprised to fall in love with a museum when I visited Roubaix, France, with some friends from the UK. They took me to the Musée du Jacquard (Jacquard Museum), which is a museum about the history of textiles. If you're ever in that part of the world, go to this museum. They give wonderful tours of the machines, which all work and which they turn on and run while explaining all about the history of textiles going back almost a thousand years.

My ears pricked up when I heard about Project Jacquard—a joint project between Google and Levi's. Clothing designers and tech designers are teaming up to weave conductive thread through articles of clothing. By touching or swiping areas of your jeans, shirt, or jacket, you'll be able to interact with software, for example, on a smartphone or any device.

SILLY OR SMART?

When I first heard about Project Jacquard, I thought it was silly. Why do we need to interface with our clothing? But as I thought about it more, I decided this might be very smart. Let's say you're driving and you want to call a contact in your smartphone. Instead of holding the smartphone in one hand and using your thumb to scroll on your smartphone, or using voice commands, how about mounting your smartphone on the dash of your car, and then just moving your hand briefly on your pants leg or your arm. Rather than reaching and trying to get your finger onto the exact target, you can tap your leg.

Does this mean, then, that people who design interfaces will also need to be fashion designers? Probably not. (Although if you're skilled in both, you should have a good career in this niche.)

It does bring up, however, the question of multi-modes. Will people be willing and able to sometimes talk to a device, for example, their smartphone, sometimes touch the device, and sometimes swipe their finger on their pants to use the same device? As long as the different modalities are easy to use and work seamlessly (pun intended), then the answer should be yes.

Takeaways

☑ As interfaces start coming in these new forms, be ready to work on multidisciplinary teams in a way you may not have before. You may be inviting a fashion designer onto one of your projects one day.

☑ With all the possibility of interaction (touch the screen, gesture near the screen, talk to the screen, move your hand over cloth), it's important to think about which modality is the best to use and when.

☑ Designing interfaces that are used on clothing requires you to focus on what are really the most important tasks and actions, for example, finding a contact name and initiating a call. Clothing interfaces are not the place for bloated feature sets.

98 PEOPLE WILL EMBRACE MIXED REALITY

Mediated, mixed, and augmented reality are related terms. They all involve changing one's perceptual view of a real-world environment. Augmented reality implies that you're adding to the physical reality, for example, when you superimpose the names of streets on your view as you look down the road wearing special glasses. Virtual reality implies that you're being immersed in a world that doesn't exist. Mixed reality is a term that implies that you may have a combination of virtual and augmented reality.

Microsoft's HoloLens in an example of a heads-up pair of glasses that allows you to see the physical world in addition to the augmented or mixed world.

Other mixed-reality devices include virtual retinal displays that project an image right onto the eye's retina. This has advantages over a headset or glasses. With a headset, the person is using his eye to see through the lens on the device. Since a virtual retinal display projects directly onto the retina, it overcomes problems such as nearsightedness.

There are other hardware technologies for mixed reality, including some that are handheld, but the heads-up type of display is most likely to be the first widespread hardware for mixed reality.

INTERACTING WITH MIXED REALITY

The way people interact with a mixed-reality space can include voice commands, but the most common type of interaction is gestures.

What will people use mixed reality for? According to Microsoft, just about anything. That may sound like marketing hype, but it may not be far off. Mixed reality combined with an app operating system means you can be free of actual screens. You can create a screen anywhere in front of you.

Note Does having augmented reality information appear on your windshield make you a better driver? Research by Mark Schall (2013) says the answer is yes, even with older drivers.

Takeaways

☑ Design becomes complicated when it occurs in space rather than on a screen. Be ready to create "screens" that are in 3-D and can be moved and enlarged to almost any size.

☑ Start thinking about applications in 3-D. Enhance your envisioning skill set to anticipate and design what people are going to want to do.

☑ Making sure that these new mixed realities are easy to navigate will be critical to their success. Speak up about usability and ease of learning.

☑ The idea of being freed from the screen is likely to resonate with people, so mixed reality may become big fast.

☑ Familiarize yourself with designing for mixed reality, as designers in this field will be in high demand.

99 OVER 645 MILLION PEOPLE HAVE VISUAL OR AUDITORY IMPAIRMENTS

A woman who is blind puts on a pair of glasses that contain a camera. The image from the camera is sent to a small device about the size of a postage stamp that sits on her tongue. She feels a sensation like soda bubbles on her tongue—this is the camera signals being sent to electrodes on her tongue. This information then goes either to the visual cortex or to the part of the brain that processes taste signals from the tongue. The scientists who developed this technology say they aren't sure which part of the brain is actually receiving the information from the tongue in this situation.

The experience of the woman when her brain receives the signals from her tongue is that she sees shapes. The vision is not the same as normal sight, but she can see enough that she can better navigate her environment. People who are totally blind can find doorways and elevator buttons when they use the device, called a BrainPort. They can read letters and numbers and pick up everyday objects, for example, a fork at the dinner table.

Note When someone uses the BrainPort at first, they don't see anything. It takes 15 minutes for them to start to interpret the signals as visual information. Interestingly, it's not that they have to "learn" anything—it's not that they are conscious of practicing. The brain is unconsciously learning to interpret the information as vision.

Until now, designing devices for people with visual, auditory, or other physical impairments has been an area that only a few designers have worked on. The rest of us have been told to make our designs "accessible" so that the special devices (such as screen readers) are compatible and can use the mainstream technologies. Keeping accessibility in mind is always important, but now more designers will be directly designing devices that are specifically created to augment the impaired sense.

Takeaways

☑ If you're a designer who has been designing for accessibility, it's time to expand your skills to include these new devices.

☑ If you're not experienced with designing for accessibility, this is a good time to learn about the new ways that devices will become accessible.

100 PEOPLE PROCESS SENSORY DATA UNCONSCIOUSLY

Jason is 20 years old and he's deaf. He puts on a special vest that's wired so that when it receives data, it sends pulses to his back.

The vest is connected to a tablet. When I say the word "book" into a microphone that feeds into the tablet, the tablet turns the word into a signal that is sent to the vest. Jason now feels a pattern on his back through his sense of touch. Initially, he can't tell you what the word is. I keep saying words and he keeps feeling the patterns. Eventually, he'll be able to tell me the words that he's hearing. His brain learns to take the pattern and translate that into words.

The interesting thing is that this happens unconsciously. He doesn't have to consciously work at learning the patterns.

This describes an actual project by David Eagleman, a neuroscientist from the Baylor College of Medicine.

It's the same idea as the BrainPort. Eagleman calls it sensory substitution. Information comes into your body and brain from your eyes, ears, touch, and so on. But did you know that the brain is actually quite flexible and plastic in this regard? When data from the environment comes in, from any of the senses, the brain figures out the best way to analyze and interpret it. Sometimes you're consciously aware of the data and its meaning, but most of the time your brain is analyzing data and using that data to make decisions, and you don't even realize it.

Note Here's a great TED Talk by Dr. Eagleman: http://www.ted.com/talks/david_eagleman_can_we_create_new_senses_for_humans.

PEOPLE CAN BEST PROCESS BIG DATA UNCONSCIOUSLY

Eagleman takes the idea of sensory substitution a step further, to sensory addition.

Eagleman has people (without hearing impairments) put on the vest. He takes stock market data and uses the same program on the tablet to turn the stock market data into patterns, and sends those patterns to the vest. The people wearing the vest don't know what the patterns are about. They don't even know it has anything to do with the stock market. He then hands them another tablet where a screen periodically appears with a big red button and a big green button.

Eagleman tells them to press a button when the colors appear. At first they have no idea why they should press one button versus the other. They're told to press a button anyway, and when they do, they get feedback about whether they're wrong or right, even though they have no idea what they are wrong or right about. The buttons are actually buy and sell decisions (red is buy, green is sell) that are related to the data they're receiving, but they don't know that.

Eventually, however, their button presses go from random to being right all the time, even though they still don't know anything consciously about the patterns.

This is sensory addition. Eagleman is essentially sending big data to people's bodies, and their brains interpret the data and make decisions from it—all unconsciously.

Big data refers to large data sets that are combed for predictive analytics. The idea is that if you can collect massive amounts of data, even disparate data, and analyze it for patterns, you can learn important information and make decisions based on that information.

Data sets of Internet searches, Twitter messages, meteorology, and more are being collected and analyzed.

But how do you convey the information in a way that makes sense? How can you get the human mind to see patterns in what at first seems like meaningless data?

The conscious thought process is not very good at this task. The conscious mind can handle only a small subset of data at one time, but the unconscious is great at taking in large amounts of data and finding patterns. If you want to see the patterns in big data, you have to engage the unconscious.

A SENSORY ROOM

Other scientists are also working on the idea. Jonathan Freeman, a professor of psychology at Goldsmiths, University of London, and Paul Verschure, a professor at the Universitat Pompeu Fabra in Barcelona, have created the eXperience Induction Machine (XIM). The XIM is a room with speakers, projectors, projection screens, pressure-sensitive floor tiles, infrared cameras, and a microphone. A person stands in the room and big data visualizations appear on the screen. Freeman and Verschure monitor the response of the person in the room through a headset. They can tell when the person is getting overloaded or tired, and then they can make the visuals simpler.

Perhaps data analysts will work in XIM rooms in the future or walk around with Eagleman's vests.

☑ Find out the percentage of people in your target audience who are likely to have auditory or visual impairments.

☑ Test your products to see if they're usable/accessible for people with visual or auditory impairments. You can run tests with people who have disabilities and you can run tests with products like screen readers to see if these devices are compatible with your product.

☑ If you don't know much about designing accessible products, check out the guidelines at http://www.w3.org/standards/webdesign/accessibility.

☑ When you're working on big data sets, use some of these new technologies to present information in non-traditional ways. Creating an infographic may not be good enough.

☑ If you're unfamiliar with big data, you may want to learn about it, because sensory addition with big data is likely to be an important design area.

☑ When you work with big data, consider the idea of bypassing complex visual analysis and how to represent the data analytically. It's probably better to feed the data directly to sense organs and let the brain do the analytics.

REFERENCES

Aaker, Jennifer, and Andy Smith. 2010. *The Dragonfly Effect: Quick, Effective, and Powerful Ways to Use Social Media to Drive Social Change*. Jossey-Bass.

Abrams, Daniel A., Srikanth Ryali, Tianwen Chen, Parag Chordia, Amirah Khouzam, Daniel J. Levitin, and Vinod Menon. 2013. "Inter-subject Synchronization of Brain Responses during Natural Music Listening." *European Journal of Neuroscience* 37(9): 1458–69. doi: 10.1111/ejn.12173.

Allport, Floyd Henry. 1920. "The Influence of the Group Upon Association and Thought." *Journal of Experimental Psychology* 3(3): 159–82. doi: 10.1037/h0067891.

Alter, Adam L., and Hal E. Hershfield. 2014. "People Search for Meaning When They Approach a New Decade in Chronological Age." *Proceedings of the National Academy of Sciences* 111(48): 17066–70. doi: 10.1073/pnas.1415086111.

Andics, Attila, Márta Gácsi, Tamás Faragó, Anna Kis, and Ádám Miklósi. 2014. "Voice-Sensitive Regions in the Dog and Human Brain Are Revealed by Comparative fMRI."*Current Biology* 24(5): 574–78. doi: 10.1016/j.cub.2014.01.058.

A. T. Kearney Omnichannel Consumer Preferences Study. https://www.atkearney.com/documents/10192/4683364/On+Solid+Ground.pdf/f96d82ce-e40c-450d-97bb-884b017f4cd7

Bar, Moshe, and Maital Neta. 2006. "Humans Prefer Curved Visual Objects." *Psychological Science* 17(8): 645–48. doi: 10.1111/j.1467-9280.2006.01759.x.

Barr, Nathaniel, Gordon Pennycook, Jennifer A. Stolz, and Jonathan A. Fugelsang. 2015. "The Brain in Your Pocket: Evidence that Smartphones Are Used to Supplant Thinking." *Computers in Human Behavior* 48: 473–80. doi: 10.1016/j.chb.2015.02.029.

Bayle, Dimitri J., Benjamin Schoendorff, Marie-Anne Hénaff, and Pierre Krolak-Salmon. 2011. "Emotional Facial Expression Detection in the Peripheral Visual Field." *PLOS One* 6(6): e21584. doi: 10.1371/journal.pone.0021584.

Berger, Jonah. 2013. *Contagious: Why Things Catch On*. Simon and Schuster.

Brown, Alan S., Lori A. Brown, and Sally L. Zoccoli, S.L. 2002. "Repetition-Based Credibility Enhancement of Unfamiliar Faces." *American Journal of Psychology* 115(2): 199–209. doi: 10.2307/1423435

Bryan, Christopher J., Gregory M. Walton, Todd Rogers, and Carol S. Dweck. 2011. "Motivating Voter Turnout by Invoking the Self." *Proceedings of the National Academy of Sciences* 108(31): 12653–12656.

Buckner, Randy L., Jessica R. Andrews-Hanna, and Daniel L. Schacter. 2008. "The Brain's Default Network Anatomy, Function, and Relevance to Disease." *New York Academy of Sciences* 1124(March): 1–38. doi: 10.1196/annals.1440.011.

Caçola, Priscila, Jerroed Roberson, and Carl Gabbard. 2013. "Aging in Movement Representations for Sequential Finger Movements: A Comparison between Young-, Middle-Aged, and Older Adults." *Brain and Cognition* 82(1): 1–5. doi: 10.1016/j.bandc.2013.02.003.

Carney, Dana R., Amy J. C. Cuddy and Andy J. Yap. 2015. "Review and Summary of Research on the Embodied Effects of Expansive (vs. Contractive) Nonverbal Displays." *Psychological Science* (May)26: 657–63. doi: 10.1177/0956797614566855.

Carr, Priyanka B., and Gregory M. Walton. (2014). "Cues of Working Together Fuel Intrinsic Motivation." *Journal of Experimental Social Psychology* 53: 169–84. doi: 10.1016/j.jesp.2014.03.015.

Chanda, Mona Lisa, and Daniel J. Levitin. 2013. "The Neurochemistry of Music." *Trends in Cognitive Sciences* 17(4): 179–93. doi: 10.1016/j.tics.2013.02.007.

Chen, Frances S., Julia A. Minson, Maren Schöne, and Markus Heinrichs. 2013. "In the Eye of the Beholder: Eye Contact Increases Resistance to Persuasion." *Psychological Science* 24(11), 2254–61. doi: 10.1177/0956797613491968.

Chow, Ho Ming, Raymond A. Mar, Yisheng Xu Siy. 2015. "Personal Experience with Narrated Events Modulates Functional Connectivity within Visual and Motor Systems during Story Comprehension." *Human Brain Mapping* 36(4): 1494–1505. doi: 10.1002/hbm.22718.

Chuong, Amy S., Mirtra L. Miri, Volker Busskamp, Gillian A. C. Matthews, Lea C. Acker, Andreas T. Sørensen, Andrew Young, Nathan C. Klapoetke, Mike A. Henninger, Suhasa B. Kodandaramaiah, Masaaki Ogawa, Shreshtha B. Ramanlal, Rachel C. Bandler, Brian D. Allen, Craig R. Forest, Brian Y. Chow, Xue Han, Yingzi Lin, Kay M. Tye, Botond Roska, Jessica A. Cardin, and Edward S. Boyden. 2014. "Noninvasive Optical Inhibition with a Red-Shifted Microbial Rhodopsin." *Nature Neuroscience* 17: 1123–29. doi: 10.1038/nn.3752.

Cwir, David, Priyanka B. Carr, Gregory M. Walton, and Steven J. Spencer. 2011. "Your Heart Makes My Heart Move: Cues of Social Connectedness Cause Shared Emotions and Physiological States among Strangers." *Journal of Experimental Social Psychology,* 47(3): 661–64. doi: 10.1016/j.jesp.2011.01.009.

Dai, Hengchen, Katherine L. Milkman, and Jason Riis. 2014. "The Fresh Start Effect: Temporal Landmarks Motivate Aspirational Behavior." *Management Science* 60(10): 2563–82. doi: 10.1287/mnsc.2014.1901.

Davis, Derick F., and Paul M. Herr. 2014. "From Bye to Buy: Homophones as a Pho-nological Route to Priming." *Journal of Consumer Research* 40(6), 1063–77. doi: 10.1086/673960.

de Gee, Jan Willem, Tomas Knapen, and Tobias H. Donner. 2014. "Decision Related Pupil Dilation Reflects Upcoming Choice and Individual Bias." *Proceedings of the National Academy of Sciences of the USA* 111(5): E618–E625. doi: 10.1073/pnas.1317557111.

Dehaene, Stanislas. 2010. *Reading in the Brain: The New Science of How We Read.* Penguin.

Deutsch, Morton, and Harold B. Gerard. 1955. "A Study of Normative and Informational Social Influences upon Individual Judgment." *Journal of Abnormal and Social Psychology* 51(3): 629–36.

de Vries, H. L. 1948. "The Fundamental Response Curves of Normal and Abnormal Dichromatic and Trichromatic Eyes." *Physica* 14(6): 367–80. doi: 10.1016/0031-8914(48)90021-4.

Diemand-Yauman, Connor, Daniel M. Oppenheimer, and Erikka B. Vaughan. 2010. "Fortune Favors the ( ): Effects of Disfluency on Educational Outcomes." *Cognition.*

Entertainment Software Association. 2014. *Essential Facts about the Computer and Video Game Industry: 2014 Sales, Demographic and Usage Data.*

Erickson, Kirk, Michelle W. Voss, Ruchika Shaurya Prakash, et al. 2014. "Exercise Training Increases Size of Hippocampus and Improves Memory." *Proceedings of the National Academy of Sciences of the United States of America* 108(7): 3017–3022. doi: 10.1073/pnas.1015950108.

Esseily, Rana, Lauriane Rat-Fischer, Eszter Somogyi, Kevin John O'Regan, and Jacqueline Fagard. 2015. "Humour Production May Enhance Observational Learning of a New Tool-Use Action in 18-Month-Old Infants." *Cognition and Emotion*, (May 12)1–9. doi: 10.1080/02699931.2015.1036840.

Festinger, Leon. 1957. *A Theory of Cognitive Dissonance.* Stanford: Stanford University Press.

Fowler, James, H. and Nicholas A Christakis. 2008. "Dynamic Spread of Happiness in a Large Social Network: Longitudinal Analysis over 20 Years in the Framingham Heart Study." *BMJ.* doi: 10.1136/bmj.a2338.

Frenda, Steven J., Eric D. Knowles, William Saletan, and Elizabeth F. Loftus. 2013. "False Memories of Fabricated Political Events." *Journal of Experimental Social Psychology* 49(2013): 280–286.

Galfano, Giovanni, Mario Dalmaso, Daniele Marzoli, Giulia Pavan, Carol Coricelli, and Luigi Castelli. 2012. "Eye Gaze Cannot Be Ignored (but Neither Can Arrows)." *Quarterly Journal of Experimental Psychology* 65(10): 1–16. doi: 10.1080/17470218.2012.663765.

Gangestad, Steven W., Leslie A. Merriman, and Melissa Emery Thompson. 2010. "Men's Oxidative Stress, Fluctuating Asymmetry, and Physical Attractiveness." *Animal Behaviour* 80(6), 1005–13. doi: 10.1016/j.anbehav.2010.09.003.

Glass, Brian D., W. Todd Maddox, and Bradley C. Love. 2013. "Real-Time Strategy Game Training: Emergence of a Cognitive Flexibility Trait. *PLOS One*, 7:8(8):e70350. doi: 10.1371/journal.pone.0070350.

Grandchamp, Romain, Claire Braboszcz, J. M. Hupé, and A. Delorme. 2011. "Pupil Dilation and Blink Rate Increase during Mind-Wandering." *Perception* 40: 144.

Gu, Yangjie, Simona Botti, and David Faro. 2013. "Turning the Page: The Impact of Choice Closure on Satisfaction." *Journal of Consumer Research* 40(2): 268–83. doi: 10.1086/670252

Haidt, Jonathan, J. Patrick Seder, and Selin Kesebir. 2008. "Hive Psychology, Happiness, and Public Policy." *Journal of Legal Studies* 37(3).

Haile, Tony. 2014. "What You Think You Know about the Web Is Wrong." http://time.com/12933/what-you-think-you-know-about-the-web-is-wrong/

Harrison, Lane, Katharina Reinecke, and Remco Chang. 2015. "Infographic Aesthetics: Designing for the First Impression." *Proceedings of the 33rd Annual ACM Conference on Human Factors in Computing Systems.* doi: 10.1145/2702123.2702545.

Hasher, Lynn, David Goldstein, and Thomas Toppino. 1977. "Frequency and the Conference of Referential Validity." *Journal of Verbal Learning and Verbal Behavior* 16(1): 107–112. doi: 10.1016/S0022-5371(77)80012-1.10.1016/S0022-5371(77)80012-1 10.1016/S0022-5371(77)80012-1 10.1016/S0022-5371(77)80012-1 10.1016/S0022-5371(77)80012-1

Hirst, William, Elizabeth A. Phelps, Robert Meksin, Chanda J. Vaidya, Marcia K. Johnson, Karen J. Mitchell, Randy L. Buckner, Andrew E. Budson, John D. Gabrieli, Cindy Lustig, Mara Mather, Kevin N. Ochsner, Daniel Schacter, Jon S. Simons, Keith B. Lyle, Alexandru F. Cuc, and Andreas Olsson. 2015. "A Ten-Year Follow-Up of a Study of Memory for the Attack of September 11, 2001: Flashbulb Memories and Memories for Flashbulb Events." *Journal of Experimental Psychology: General* (144)3: 604–23. doi: 10.1037/xge0000055.

Hoober, Steven. 2014. "The Rise of the Phablet: Designing for Larger Phones." *UX Matters*. http://www.uxmatters.com/mt/archives/2014/11/the-rise-of-the-phablet-designing-for-larger-phones.php.

Howes, Mary J., Jack E. Hokanson, and David A. Loewenstein. 1985. "Induction of Depressive Affect after Prolonged Exposure to a Mildly Depressed Individual." *Journal of Personality and Social Psychology*, 49(4): 1110–3.

Intel. 2012. *Women and the web*. http://www.intel.com/content/dam/www/public/us/en/documents/pdf/women-and-the-web.pdf.

Isaksen, Scott G., and John P. Gaulin. 2005. "A Reexamination of Brainstorming Research: Implications for Research and Practice." *Gifted Child Quarterly* 49(4): 315–329. doi: 10.1177/001698620504900405.

Jabr, Ferris. 2013. "The Reading Brain in the Digital Age: The Science of Paper Versus Screens." http://www.scientificamerican.com/article/reading-paper-screens/

Jeffries, Adrienne. 2014. "You're Not Going to Read This." http://www.theverge.com/2014/2/14/5411934/youre-not-going-to-read-this

Ji, Daoyun, and Matthew Wilson. 2007. "Coordinated Memory Replay in the Visual Cortex and Hippocampus during Sleep." *Nature Neuroscience* 10: 100–107. doi: 10.1038/nn1825.

Kabali, Hilda, Rosemary Nunez-Davis, Sweta Mohanty, Jennifer Budacki, Kristin Leister, Maria Katrina Tan, Matilde Irigoyen, and Robert Bonner. 2015. *First Exposure and Use of Mobile Media in Young Children*. Pediatrics, Einstein Medical Center Philadelphia, Philadelphia, PA.

Kahneman, Daniel. 2013. *Thinking, Fast and Slow*. Farrar, Straus and Giroux.

Kiani, Roozbeh, Leah Corthell, and Michael N. Shadlen. 2014. "Choice Certainty Is Informed by Both Evidence and Decision Time" *Neuron* 84(6): 1329–42. doi: 10.1016/j.neuron.2014.12.015

Kramer, Adam D. I., Jamie E. Guillory, and Jeffrey T. Hancock. 2014. "Experimental Evidence of Massive-Scale Emotional Contagion through Social Networks." *Proceedings of the National Academy of Sciences of the USA* 111(24): 8788–90. doi: 10.1073/pnas.1320040111.

Krug, Steve. 2014. *Don't Make Me Think*. New Riders, 3rd ed.

Leder, Helmut, Pablo P. L. Tinio, and Moshe Bar. 2011. "Emotional Valence Modulates the Preference for Curved Objects." *Perception* 40(6): 649–55. doi: 10.1068/p6845.

Levitin, Daniel J. 2014. *The Organized Mind: Thinking Straight in the Age of Information Overload*. Dunnon.

Looser, Christine E., and Thalia Wheatley. (2010). "The Tipping Point of Animacy: How, When, and Where We Perceive Life in a Face." *Psychological Science* 21(12): 1854–62. doi: 10.1177/0956797610388044.

Ludwig, Casimir J. H., J. Rhys Davies, and Miguel P. Eckstein. 2014. "Foveal Analysis and Peripheral Selection during Active Visual Sampling." *Proceedings of the National Academy of Sciences of the USA* 111(2): E291–E299. doi: 10.1073/pnas.1313553111.

Mack, Michael L., Alison R. Preston, and Bradley C. Love. 2013. "Decoding the Brain's Algorithm for Categorization from Its Neural Implementation." *Current Biology* 23(20): 2023–27. doi: 10.1016/j.cub.2013.08.035.

Mangen, Anne, Bente R. Walgermo, and Kolbjørn Brønnick. 2013. "Reading Linear Texts on Paper Versus Computer Screen: Effects on Reading Comprehension." *International Journal of Educational Research* 58: 61-68. doi: 10.1016/j.ijer.2012.12.002.

Margulis, Elizabeth Hellmuth. 2013. *On Repeat: How Music Plays the Mind*. Oxford University Press.

Mather, Mara, and Nichole R. Lighthall. 2012. "Both Risk and Reward Are Processed Differently in Decisions Made Under Stress." *Current Directions in Psychological Science* 21(1): 36–41. doi: 10.1177/0963721411429452.

McMillan, Rebecca L., Scott Barry Kaufman, and Jerome L. Singer. 2013. "Ode to Positive Constructive Daydreaming." *Frontier in Psychology*. doi: 10.3389/fpsyg.2013.00626.

Mehler, Bruce. 2015. *Multi-Modal Demands of a Smartphone Used to Place Calls and Enter Addresses during Highway Driving Relative to Two Embedded Systems*. MIT AgeLab.

Mehta, Ravi, Juliet Zhu Rui, and Amar Cheema. 2012. "Is Noise Always Bad? Exploring the Effects of Ambient Noise on Creative Cognition." *Journal of Consumer Research* 29(4).

Menon, Vinod, and Bressler, S.L. 2010. "Large-Scale Brain Networks in Cognition: Emerging Methods and Principles." *Trends in Cognitive Science* 14(6): 277–90.

Mikels, Joseph A., E. Cheung, J. Cone, and T. Gilovich, T. 2013. "The Dark Side of Intuition: Aging and Increases in Nonoptimal Intuitive Decisions." *Emotion* 13(2): 189–95. doi: 10.1037/a0030441.

Mikels, Joseph A., Sam J. Maglio, Andrew E. Reed, and Lee J. Kaplowitz. 2011. *Emotion* 11(4): 743–53.

Milosavljevic, Milica, Vidhya Navalpakkam, Christof Koch, and Antonio Rangel. 2012. "Relative Visual Saliency Differences Induce Sizable Bias in Consumer Choice." *Journal of Consumer Psychology* 22(1).

Milosavljevic, Milica, Christof Koch, and Antonio Rangel. 2011. "Consumers Can Make Decisions in as Little as a Third of a Second." *Judgment and Decision Making* 6(6): 520–30.

Mori, Masahiro. 2012. *The Uncanny Valley*. Trans. Karl F. MacDorman and Norri Kageki. IEEE Spectrum. http://spectrum.ieee.org/automaton/robotics/humanoids/the-uncanny-valley>.

Nakamura, Kimihiro, Wen-Jui Kuo, Felipe Pegade, Laurent Cohen, Ovid J.L. Tzeng, and Stanislas Dehaene. 2012. "Universal Brain Systems for Recognizing Word Shapes and Handwriting Gestures during Reading." *Proceedings of the National Academy of Sciences of the USA* 109(50).

Nantais, Kristin M., and E. Glenn Schellenberg. 1999. "The Mozart Effect: An Artifact of Preference." *Psychological Science* 10(4).

Newman, Erin J., M. Garry, C. Bernstein, D.S. Lindsay, and R.A. Nash. 2015. "Truthiness and Falsiness of Trivia Claims Depend on Judgmental Contexts." *Journal of Experimental Psychology: Learning, Memory, and Cognition.*

Pavel, Amy, Colorado Reed, Bjoern Hartmann, and Maneesh Agrawala. 2014. "Video Digests: A Browsable, Skimmable Format for Informational Lecture Videos." *Proceedings of the 27th Annual ACM Symposium on User Interface Software and Technology.* 573–82.

Pew Research Center American Trends Survey. October 2014.

Pew Research Center Survey. 2000–2015.

Przybylski, Andrew K., and Netta Weinstein. 2013. "Can You Connect with Me Now? How the Presence of Mobile Communication Technology Influences Face-to-Face Conversation Quality." *Journal of Social and Personal Relationships* 30(3): 237–246.

Ratcliffe, Victoria F., and David Reby. 2014. "Orienting Asymmetries in Dogs' Responses to Different Communicatory Components of Human Speech." *Current Biology* 24(24): 2908–12.

Reber, Rolf, and Norbert Schwarz. 1999. "Effects of Perceptual Fluency on Judgments of Truth." *Consciousness and Cognition* 8: 338–42.

Reed, Andrew E., Joseph A. Mikels, and Corinna E. Lockenhoff. 2013. "Preferences for Choice across Adulthood: Age Trajectories and Potential Mechanisms." *Psychology and Aging* 28(3): 625–32.

Reimer, Bryan, Bruce Mehler, Ian Reagan, David Kidd, and Jonathan Dobres. 2015. "Multi-Modal Demands of a Smartphone Used to Place Calls and Enter Addresses during Highway Driving Relative to Two Embedded Systems." http://www.iihs.org/frontend/iihs/documents/masterfiledocs.ashx?id=2088.

Reinecke, Katharina, and Gajos Krzysztof. 2014. "Quantifying Visual Preferences around the World." *Proceedings of the 33rd Annual ACM Conference on Human Factors in Computing Systems.*

Reinecke, Katharina, Tom Yeh, Luke Miratrix, Rahmatri Mardiko, Yuechen Zhao, Jenny Liu, and Krzysztof Z. Gajos. 2013. "Predicting Users' First Impressions of Website Aesthetics With a Quantification of Perceived Visual Complexity and Colorfulness." *Proceedings of the 33rd Annual ACM Conference on Human Factors in Computing Systems.*

Rigby, Darrell. 2014. "E-Commerce Is Not Eating Retail." *Harvard Business Review*. https://hbr.org/2014/08/e-commerce-is-not-eating-retail/.

Rosenthal-von der Pütten, Astrid Marieke, Frank P. Schulte, Sabrina C. Eimler, Laura Hoffmann, Sabrina Sobieraj, Stefan Maderwald, Nicole C. Kramer, and Matthias Brand. 2013. "Neural Correlates of Empathy towards Robots." *Proceedings of the 8th ACM/IEEE International Conference on Human-Robot Interaction*. 215-216.

Sawyer, Keith. 2013. *Zig Zag: The Surprising Path to Greater Creativity*. Jossey-Bass.

Schall, Mark, Michelle Rusch, John Lee, Jeffrey Dawson, Geb Thomas, Nazan Aksan, and Matthew Rizzo. 2013. "Augmented Reality Cues and Elderly Driver Hazard Perception." *Human Factors: The Journal of the Human Factors and Ergonomics Society* 55: 643–58.

Shadmehr, Reza, and Henry H. Holcomb. 1997. "Neural Correlates of Memory Motor Consolidation." *Science* 277(5327): 821–25. doi: 10.1126/science.277.5327.821.

Shepherd, Kathrine, and Moshe Bar. 2011. "Preference for Symmetry: Only on Mars?" *Perception* 40: 1254–56.

Silvia, Paul J., and Christopher M. Barona. 2009. "Do People Prefer Curved Objects? Angularity, Expertise, and Aesthetic Preference." *Empirical Studies of the Arts* 27(1): 25-42.

Soon, Chun Siong, Anna Hanxi He, Stefan Bode, and John-Dylan Haynes. 2013. "Predicting Free Choices for Abstract Intentions." *Proceedings of the National Academy of Sciences of the USA* 110(15). doi: 10.1073/.1212218110.

Soon, Chun Siong, Marcel Brass, Hans-Jochen Heinze, and John-Dylan Haynes. 2008. "Unconscious Determinants of Free Decisions in the Human Brain." *Nature Neuroscience* 11(5). doi: 10.1038/nn.2112.

Stephens, Greg, Lauren J. Silbert, and Uri Hasson. 2010. "Speaker–Listener Neural Coupling Underlies Successful Communication." *Proceedings of the National Academy of Science* 107(32): 14425–30. doi: 10.1073/pnas.1008662107.

Teixeira, Thales. 2012. "The New Science of Viral Ads." *Harvard Business Review*.

Thornton, Bill, Ayson Faires, Maija Robbins, and Eric Rollins. 2014. "The Mere Presence of a Cell Phone May Be Distracting: Implications for Attention and Task Performance." *Social Psychology* 45(6): 479–88. doi: 10.1027/1864-9335/a000216.

Touron, Dayna. 2015. "Memory Avoidance by Older Adults: When 'Old Dogs' Won't Perform Their 'New Tricks." *Current Directions in Psychological Science* 24(3): 170–76. doi: 10.1177/0963721414563730.

Tversky, Amos, and Daniel Kahneman. 1974. "Judgment under Uncertainty: Heuristics and Biases." *Science* 185(4157): 1124–31. doi: 10.1126/science

Vickhoff, Björn, Helge Malmgren, Rickard Åström, Gunnar Nyberg, Seth-Reino Ekströ, Mathias Engwall, Johan Snygg, Michael Nilsson, and Rebecka Jörnsten. 2013. "Music Structure Determines Heart Rate Variability of Singers." *Frontiers in Psychology 4:334.* doi: 10.3389/fpsyg.2013.00334

Walton, Gregory M., Geoffrey Cohen, David Cwir, and Steven Spencer. 2012. "Mere Belonging: The Power of Social Connections." *Journal of Personality and Social Psychology* 102(3): 513–32. doi: 10.1037/a0025731.

Walton, Gregory M., and Banaji, Mahzarin. 2004. "Being What You Say: The Effect of Essentialist Linguistic Labels on Preferences." *Social Cognition* 22(2): 193–213.

Waytz, Adam, Joy Heafner, and Nicholas Epley. 2014. "The Mind in the Machine: Anthropomorphism Increases Trust in an Autonomous Vehicle." *Journal of Experimental Social Psychology*, 52, 113–117. doi: 10.1016/j.jesp.2014.01.005.

Wilson, Timothy. 2011. *Redirect: The Surprising New Science of Psychological Change.* Little Brown and Company.

Wiltermuth, Scott, and C. Heath. 2009. "Synchrony and Cooperation." *Psychological Science* 20(1): 1–5. doi: 10.1111/j.1467-9280.2008.02253.

Wolf, Maryanne. 2008. *Proust and the Squid: The Story and Science of the Reading Brain.* Harper Perennial.

Woodson, Wesley, Peggy Tillman, and Barry Tillman. 1992. *Human Factors Design Handbook, 2nd edition.* (3rd edition due out in 2016).

Xiong, Jinghong, and Satoshi Muraki. 2014. "An Ergonomics Study of Thumb Movements on Smartphone Touch Screen." *Ergonomics* 943-955. doi: 10.1080/00140139.2014.904007.

Zak, Paul. 2013 *The Moral Molecule.* Plume.

INDEX